D0952597

Rendezvous with Oblivion

RENDEZVOUS
WITH
OBLIVION

REPORTS FROM A SINKING SOCIETY

Thomas Frank

METROPOLITAN BOOKS
HENRY HOLT AND COMPANY   NEW YORK

Metropolitan Books
Henry Holt and Company
Publishers since 1866
175 Fifth Avenue
New York, New York 10010
www.henryholt.com

Metropolitan Books® and ® are registered trademarks of
Macmillan Publishing Group, LLC.

Distributed in Canada by Raincoast Book Distribution Limited

Library of Congress Cataloging-in-Publication Data

Names: Frank, Thomas, 1965– author.
Title: Rendezvous with oblivion : reports from a sinking society / Thomas Frank.
Description: First edition. | New York : Metropolitan Books, Henry Holt and
    Company, 2018.
Identifiers: LCCN 2017060877 | ISBN 9781250293664 (hardcover)
Subjects: LCSH: Political culture—United States. | Polarization (Social
    sciences)—United States.
Classification: LCC JK1726 .F665 2018 | DDC 306.20973—dc23
LC record available at https://lccn.loc.gov/2017060877

Our books may be purchased in bulk for promotional, educational, or
business use. Please contact your local bookseller or the Macmillan Corporate and
Premium Sales Department at (800) 221-7945, extension 5442, or by e-mail
at MacmillanSpecialMarkets@macmillan.com.

First Edition 2018

Designed by Kelly S. Too

Printed in the United States of America

1 3 5 7 9 10 8 6 4 2

CONTENTS

Rendezvous with Oblivion

INTRODUCTION

The First Shall Be First

The essays collected here scan over many diverse aspects of American life, but they all aim to tell one essential story: This is what a society looks like when the glue that holds it together starts to dissolve. This is the way ordinary citizens react when they learn the structure beneath them is crumbling. This is the thrill that pulses through the veins of the well-to-do when they discover there is no longer any limit on their power to accumulate.

In headline terms, these essays cover the years of the Barack Obama presidency and the populist explosion that marked its end. It was a time when liberal hopes were sinking and the newly invigorated right was proceeding from triumph to triumph. When I wrote the earliest installment in the collection, Democrats still technically controlled both houses of Congress in addition to the presidency; when I finished these essays, Donald Trump sat in the Oval Office and Republicans had assumed a position of almost unprecedented power over the nation's political system.

For a few, these were times of great personal satisfaction. The effects of what was called the Great Recession were receding, and affluence had returned to smile once again on the tasteful and the fortunate. The lucky ones resumed their fascinating inquiries into the art of the cocktail and the science of the grandiose suburban home. For them, things transpired reassuringly as before.

But for the many, this was a period when reassurance was in short supply. Ordinary Americans began to understand that, recovery or not, things would probably never be the same in their town or neighborhood. For them, this was a time of cascading collapse, with one trusted institution after another visibly deteriorating.

It was a golden age of corruption. By this I do not mean that our top political leaders were on the take—they weren't—but rather that America's guardian class had been subverted or put to sleep. Human intellect no longer served the interests of the public; it served money—or else it ceased to serve at all. That was the theme of the era, whether the locale was Washington, D.C., or the college your kids attended, or the city desk of your rapidly shrinking local newspaper. No one was watching out for the interests of the people, and increasingly the people could see that this was the case.

The financial crisis of 2008 engraved this pattern in the public mind. Every trusted professional group touching the mortgage industry had turned out to be corrupt: real estate appraisers had puffed the housing bubble, credit rating agencies had puffed Wall Street's trashy securities, and of course investment bankers themselves had created the financial instruments that were designed to destroy their clients. And then, as the larger economy spiraled earthward . . . as millions around the world lost jobs and homes . . . the trusted professionals of the federal government stepped in to ensure that their brother professionals on Wall Street would suffer no ill effects. For the present generation, the bailout of the crooks would stand as the ultimate demonstration of the worthlessness of institutions, the nightmare knowledge that lurked behind every scam that was to come.

What I describe in this volume is a vast panorama of such scams—a republic of rip-offs. Bernie Sanders, the archetypal reform figure of our time, likes to say that "the business model of Wall Street is fraud," but in truth we could say that about many of the designated protectors of our health and well-being. Pharmaceutical companies, we learned, jack up prices for no reason other than because they can, because it is their federally guaranteed right to do so. The brain power of Silicon Valley, meanwhile, concentrates on the search for ingenious ways to harvest private information and build monopolies so that it, too, can gouge the world with impunity.

The university is the ultimate source of credentialed expertise—of the idea that there are values beyond those of the market—and here, too, the rot and the corruption were unmistakable. That the traditional professoriate was doomed became obvious in these years, and also that the contemplative way of life was circling the drain as well. But even as the intellectuals went down, the universities themselves prospered in a remarkable and even unprecedented way, growing and building and driving tuition prices skyward. As these developments unfolded, legitimate higher ed was dogged by countless educational scams and even fake-educational scams, operations that would sell anyone a realistic-looking college degree for a modest sum.

In politics, of course, the scam and the fib are as old as the earth itself. Even so, the past decade has been a time of extraordinary innovation in the field. The rise of the super PAC and the *Citizens United* decision drew the most attention in this regard, but what seems most striking in retrospect was the way the casual dishonesty of politics started to spill over into everyday life.

The consolations of ideology became available to the millions, thanks to Facebook and Twitter and the political entertainers on cable news. Millions of Americans came to believe that everything was political and that therefore everything was faked; that everyone was a false accuser so why not accuse people falsely; that any complaint or objection could ultimately be confounded by some clever meme; that they or their TV heroes had discovered the made-up argument by which they could drown out that still small voice of reality. At right-wing rallies, one began to notice a gleeful denial of things that were obviously true.

Legitimate public defenders like newspapers were simply shutting down. And as your local paper went silent, the reign of factuality seemed to crumble as well. Among newspapers that survived, meanwhile, the resident professionals often seemed to be in denial about what was happening. This was a "golden age of journalism," they chanted, and as their little world shrank and the public grew to hate them more and more, the survivors came together in an ever tighter circle of professional unanimity, missing the obvious but agreeing with one another on the correct interpretation of an amazing variety of events.

Fake news flourished, of course. For every newspaper that withered away, an opportunity opened up for somebody willing to imitate what had gone before. Social media entrepreneurs prospered, as did home-grown propagandists and online scam artists. It sometimes seemed as if everyone was search-engine-optimizing something or making bogus documentaries or Photoshopping some outrageous text onto some stock photo. The Internet teemed with collators of tweets, makers of memes, content farms, traffickers in panic and stereotype, liars for hire.

The representative figure of this new era was Andrew Breitbart, the master of a homemade right-wing Web empire, who rose from obscurity to become the bellowing scourge of the mainstream media: accusing promiscuously, denying vociferously, always shouting, always rationalizing. For him, representation was everything, reality was nothing, and politics became more and more an analogue of pro wrestling. The pseudo-event was the only game in town.

The United States has always been friendly to quacks and mountebanks and false accusers; that is an essential teaching of this country's literature from the days of Mark Twain to those of Lewis Lapham. Like pumpkin pie and the bald eagle, the con game is so utterly American that it probably deserves its own series of postage stamps. But something is different today. The quacks and the mountebanks own the place, and everyone knows it. The con game is our national pastime. Everyone either is in on it or has a plan for getting in on it soon.

What has made corruption's reign possible is no mystery. For most Americans, the props of middle-class life—four years at college, for example—are growing expensive and moving out of reach. At the same time, the rewards showered upon society's handful of winners have grown astronomically greater. The result is exactly what our cynical ancestors would have expected: people will do anything to be among the winners.

And as we serve money, we find that money always wants the same thing from us: that it pushes everyone it beguiles in the same direction. Money never seems to be interested in strengthening regulatory agencies, for example, but always in subverting them, in making them miss the danger signs in coal mines and in derivatives trading and in deep-sea oil wells. You can have a shot at joining the one percent, money tells us, only if you are first committed to making the one percent stronger, to defending their piles in some new and imaginative way, to rationalizing and burnishing their glory, to exempting them from regulation or taxation and bowing down as they pass.

What I am describing is not "sustainable," as people in Washington like to say. It has given us a rendezvous with oblivion, not with destiny. You can't build a civilization on rip-offs . . . on no-doc loans taken out in order to make scam phone calls to senior citizens . . . on rolled-back odometers and fancy college degrees that are worth less than they used to be and might well prove to be worthless altogether . . . on the presidential aspirations of a con man who mimics your way of talking but has no idea how to govern.

And so we come to Donald Trump, the very personification of this low, dishonest age. Nearly every one of the trends described in this book culminates with him. He is an Ivy League graduate who also went into business selling degrees of his own. A dealer in tasteless palatial real estate. A one-man right-wing propaganda bureau who didn't seem to be able to distinguish between what was true and what was false amid his constant tweetings and accusings. A character from pro wrestling and reality TV. A true-believing adherent of Breitbart's doctrine that only media matters—indeed, a candidate whose 2016 campaign was run by the viceroy of Breitbart's empire.

Trump was the most virulent fake populist of them all: a "blue-collar billionaire," as his admirers described him, a Republican who was carried to victory by his lovable habit of inventing cruel nicknames for his opponents. The legitimate media came together against him as a matter of course, tallying up his falsehoods and insults and assuring their audience that he represented the end of conservatism at long last. The country's surviving newspapers endorsed his Democratic opponent by an unprecedented margin.

For all that, there was still something real about Trump— or rather about the suffering of the white working-class people who attended his rallies and who made him their president during the crazy election of 2016. These were people on the receiving end of the trends I've described; they were living in the world dominated by the self-serving professionals who screwed things up and survived to screw things up again. Despite what the Beltway types assured them, they knew that the wars were inexcusable and the elites were corrupt and the trade deals were bad. And what others saw as Trump's falsehoods they saw as a form of honesty, a plain-speaking directness that was refreshing in all its vulgarity. They looked not to be saved by experts but rescued from them, and Trump's achievement was to make himself the vehicle of their hopes.

The results were disastrous, of course, and much of what I

describe in the book that follows are matters of grave import. You will notice, however, that I describe them with a certain amount of levity. I do that because that's the only way to confront the issues of our time without sinking into debilitating gloom. "We live in a land of abounding quackeries," wrote H. L. Mencken once upon a time, "and if we do not learn how to laugh we succumb to the melancholy disease which afflicts the race of viewers-with-alarm."

PART 1

MANY VIBRANT MANSIONS

Servile Disobedience

Social scientists have tried for more than a century to understand how class works. Psychological experiments on the subject, however, are a relatively novel thing. So I was surprised to
discover a few years ago that psychologists had published a series
of papers on the behavioral aspects of social status—and that
their findings were almost uniformly unflattering toward society's winners.

One 2009 study in *Psychological Science* found that, in conver-
sations with strangers, higher-status people tend to do more
doodling and fidgeting and also to use fewer "engagement
cues"—looking at the other person, laughing, and nodding their
heads. A 2010 paper published in the *Journal of Personality and
Social Psychology* found that "lower-class individuals" turned out
to be better performers on measures of such "prosocial" virtues
as generosity, charity, and helpfulness. A third study found that

those of higher status were noticeably worse at assessing the emotions of others or figuring out what facial expressions meant.

All of which is to say, the rich are different from you and me. They are more rude and less generous. They don't get what others are thinking. And apparently they don't really care.

Perhaps this is obvious to you. After all, people don't design toxic debt obligations by calling on what they learned in Sunday school. Still, the research aroused media interest. The *Christian Science Monitor's* 2010 account of one study ended with this quotation from Michael Kraus, then of the University of California, San Francisco, who was one of the researchers:

> Being empathic is one of the first steps to helping other people. . . . One of the first things we're really interested in is what can make wealthy people—affluent people, the people with the largest capacity to give—what can make them empathic?

I think I see the urgency of Dr. Kraus's question. After all, we have spent the past several decades doing everything we could to transfer the wealth of the nation into the bank accounts of the affluent, to send them victorious, happy and glorious, long to reign over us.

Oh, we've cut their taxes, gladly transferring much of the cost of keeping their property safe onto our own shoulders. We've furnished them with special megaphones so that their voices might be heard over the hubbub of the crowd. We have conferred upon them separate and better schools, their very own transportation system, and a full complement of private security guards. We've built an entire culture of courtiers and syco-phants to make their every waking hour an otherworldly delight.

We let them construct a system of bonuses and "executive compensation" on the theory that it would be good for everyone if the people on top got to take home much, much more than the rest of us. And when it turned out that the theory was wrong—that in the most famous cases, executives chased bonuses not to the shareholders' benefit but at their expense—why, we promptly bailed them out. We allowed them to step up to the Fed's dis-count window and fill their pockets, we generously transferred their reckless investments to our balance sheet, and we chas-tised them with little more than a polite request that they please not do it again. We've done everything we can to lift them up and exalt them as a new Leviathan; the least they can do in return, one feels, is show a little empathy.

Besides, look what we've done with the old Leviathan, the government. For decades we have attacked it, redirected it, out-sourced it, and filled it with incompetents and cronies. Yes, it still works well enough when we need it to blow up some small country, but those branches of it designed to help out Ameri-cans of "lower socioeconomic status," as the scientists would put it, are now bare.

We need the rich to be nice. We need them to stop doodling, pay attention, and get generous. Now that the government has divested from the empathy business, we need the rich to dis-cover brotherly love, and fast.

Come to think of it, wasn't that supposed to be the deal in the first place, the arrangement Andrew Carnegie brokered over a century ago, when he made his big career move from steel king to public-library baron? The laissez-faire social contract would grant private business a free hand, but in exchange those who piled up massive wealth were supposed to extend a magnanimous hand to the rest of us. As Carnegie wrote in his famous 1889 essay, "The Gospel of Wealth," we didn't need socialism to solve our problems; philanthropy is "the true antidote for the temporary unequal distribution of wealth, the reconciliation of the rich and the poor." Going further, Carnegie argued that the "duty of the man of wealth" was

> to consider all surplus revenues which come to him simply as trust funds, which he is called upon to administer in the manner which, in his judgment, is best calculated to produce the most beneficial results for the community—the man of wealth thus becoming the mere trustee and agent for his poorer brethren.

The same way of thinking led Carnegie to support the estate tax—"of all forms of taxation this seems the wisest," he wrote. It was wise because it would "induce the rich man to attend to the administration of wealth during his life," and if he didn't, then the tax would return most of his hoardings to the "community from which it chiefly came."

Vestiges of the Carnegie attitude survive to this day. A 2009 study of high-net-worth individuals by Barclays Wealth ("a leading global wealth manager") confirmed that American philanthropists tend to understand their giving in a context in which the state is either absent or irrelevant.

And, of course, there are plenty of nice plutocrats who don't fidget or doodle when talking to strangers, and who have no problem endowing a ward or a wing in return for a commemorative plaque. The business headlines even occasionally tell of billionaires coming together under the leadership of Warren Buffett and Bill Gates to donate their fortunes to worthy causes.

But the billionaires with the strongest sense of class solidarity have a very different plan for their disposable income: activating their lobbyists in Washington, building grassroots movements to march on their behalf, and using their media properties to run experiments on human credulity.

Even their giving is a form of taking. In 2010, for example, Charles Koch, of Wichita oil fame, circulated to his "network of business and philanthropic leaders" an invitation to a meeting at which—if their previous meeting's agenda is any indication— they were to discuss strategies for beating back environmentalism and the "threat" of financial regulation. This is a kind of philanthropy that pays dividends.

If the affluent no longer possess the capacity to interpret facial expressions, let alone maintain a social conscience, can we find a way, with the help of behavioral economics, to make them act as if they do? One idea out there is to turn the rich, via a little marketing jujitsu that exploits their well-known taste for prestigious consumer goods, into supporters of more benevolent trends. The means by which this might be done were actually the subject of a 2010 study on "green" consumerism by a psychologist and two marketing professors.

Summarizing their results in the *Journal of Personality and Social Psychology,* the academics announced that "activating status motives" can push people to choose environmentally friendly products over luxury goods and thereby ensnare consumers in a race to niceness that the scholars call "competitive altruism." The conditions have to be just right, of course. People will pay more for a green product, the researchers found, if they are buying it in public, where everybody can see them doing it. They will also be drawn to "prosocial" products if the prices are artificially high; that way their sacrifice will be especially acute and their status bump that much more noticeable. The preeminent example of such behavior, the scholars tell us, is the Toyota Prius, a hybrid car that "essentially functions as a mobile, self-promoting billboard for proenvironmentalism."

All that remains is to give the rich some form of psychic gratification that can outweigh the profits that would come from their usual routine. At one of Warren Buffett's gatherings of the superwealthy, according to a 2010 issue of *Fortune* magazine, a number of such inducements were discussed: "national recognition of great philanthropists (presidential medals, for example), or a film, or a philanthropy guidebook." The idea Buffett's group finally settled upon was to get billionaires to pledge to give 50 percent of their riches to charity. (What is now called the Giving Pledge has since been taken by more than 170 people.)

Another approach would be to leverage the human accessories that are so much in vogue these days—in Hollywood, nothing says "*I care*" like adopting a war orphan. And so perhaps we can, with some deft cultural manipulation, make it equally rewarding for a billionaire to adopt, say, the entire blue-collar population of Rockford, Illinois. The city can rename itself in the billionaire's honor, and in return all the kids might get college educations and a start in some industry other than fastener manufacturing.

But then there's the bummer backlash that inevitably over-takes all such plans. What happens to green consumerism, for example, when all those canny shoppers figure out that market-ers are making high-minded things expensive just to trigger the buyer's status anxiety? What will those consumers do when it becomes plain how absurd it is to show off by wearing $120 Fair Trade hemp tennis shoes, or when their pretensions to thrift expose them to the derision of consumers even more environ-mentally savvy than themselves? How will they react when they discover that those hair shirts aren't really trendy at all, just uncomfortable? What happens when they figure out that altru-ism isn't really in their self-interest?

Among those who make it their business to manipulate the atti-tudes of the rich, one of the hottest trends these days is the zero option: the belief that what the rich owe the rest of us is abso-lutely nothing.

Attend a few Tea Party rallies around the country and you'll inevitably be passed a platter of the novelist Ayn Rand's spiciest hors d'oeuvres. She is hot stuff these days. True, it was her phi-losophy of market rationality and bankerly heroism that guided the disastrous policymaking of the conservatives who brought us to economic ruin, and it was even a former member of her inner circle, Alan Greenspan, who personally prescribed much of the snake oil, but by the curious homeopathy of American politics that merely means we need a larger dose of the same poison; it means Ms. Rand is the rightest dame who ever lived.

Back in her heyday, Rand would occasionally address audi-ences of businessmen, exhorting them to understand that they had few moral obligations to others. Altruism, she told one such gathering in 1981, was "a contemptibly evil idea" promulgated by guilt-slinging "humanitarians" in order to shake down the productive. Insofar as they accepted this "altruism," the business class committed "treason against themselves." And so the novelist inveighed against philanthropic donations to universities, where altruists twisted the minds of the young. "It is a moral crime to give money to support your own destroyers," she scolded.

In her 1957 novel *Atlas Shrugged*, Rand also proposed a famous antidote to all this mawkish nonsense: a union of class-conscious plutocrats that would go on strike and bring the world to its knees. *Atlas Shrugged* is celebrated as a prophetic book, and in certain ways Ms. Rand's imagined future has come to pass. After all, what is the phrase "too big to fail" but a standing threat to shut down the system unless the firm in question gets its way? In 2008, Wall Street essentially held the nation's 401(k)s hostage until it was bailed out. And in 2011, the pet political party of business essentially held the legislative process itself hostage until its favorite tax cuts were extended.

As both rejoinder and homage to Ayn Rand, let us consider a different sort of strike, one that might help the emotionally arrested rich in their time of need. I propose a twenty-four-hour refusal to fawn. A servility strike. A day without deference.

For one day, let the nation's doormen do their jobs without smiling. Let waiters at suburban restaurants leave their flair at home; let waiters at downtown restaurants neglect to compliment the good taste of their customers. Let the janitors at Princeton mop no vomit from the dormitory stairwells. Let retail greeters of every description call in sick. Let the first-class passengers board at someone else's leisure. Let the nation's limo drivers require their passengers to open their own damn doors. Let the production interns at CNBC send the on-air "talent" to fetch the coffee. And, for just one day, let the talent ask their interviewees hard questions.

It wouldn't change much, of course. It would do nothing to alter the economic system that produced all those affluent louts in the first place, or the way that system divvies up what we produce, suborns the state, sends your job to China, and smashes your retirement fund for good measure. A day without deference will do nothing to fix the faithless machinery that assembles winners in its own churlish image. But as a form of therapy for those winners, it might just work. It might help them to actualize their true selves, overcome their inner barriers to sharing. And maybe that's what vast industrial actions ought to be about in the first place.

After all, Americans are born to serve and assist the wealthy; it is our inalienable duty. We like to think of ourselves as a people of untamed independence, but any observer not steeped in our culture would quickly conclude that we are a nation of footmen. We cater to the wealthy in our work lives and we glorify them in our leisure time. Our dueling political parties are dedicated to the principle of serving them, and even our seething anti-elitist movements, such as the Tea Party, are designed to build even further the affluence of the affluent. We elect politicians who slice away at the estate tax because we feel the fortunes of the rich ought to go unencumbered by that burden. Our leaders in Washington are perennially considering cutting Social Security because retaining it might require the rich to chip in more than their current percentage. If it's a choice between us spending our dotage in helplessness and filth and our high-net-worth friends having to forgo next year's Learjet, Americans will choose the personal sacrifice every time.

By withholding niceness for a day we might, surprisingly, inculcate niceness in our charges. So let's teach the rich to listen. Not because we have anything interesting to say, of course. Not for our own sake. But for theirs.

(2011)

The Architecture of Inequality

My first memorable encounter with what we now call the McMansion came somewhere around 1985. I was reclining comfortably under a concrete bridge on what were then the fringes of the Kansas City metro area, drinking beer with my alienated friends and (if memory serves) listening to Hüsker Dü's *Zen Arcade* on a boom box. In the twilight distance, we could see a housing development going up—by which I mean a development of enormous piles, dozens of houses that were all far larger than the postwar ranches and split-levels that were then so familiar to us.

Kansas City has always been a significant locale in the history of suburbia, thanks to the heroic labors of a few local developers, and as the eighties passed I became fascinated with the grandiose turn that sprawl was taking. I drove around, photographing and even walking through the yawning new homes on open-house days. What intrigued me then was the undisguised pretentiousness that accompanied the whole gaudy business. I visited a neighborhood called Patrician Woods. I took pictures of houses that seemed to have been designed by Stanford White after a debilitating brain injury. In 1990, I illustrated an issue of my magazine, the *Baffler,* with preposterous home designs clipped from a local real estate agency's catalog. Har har har.

What I didn't understand at the time was that these ostentatious new developments were a product not of some epidemic of vulgarity but of the larger economic changes in the world. By this I do not mean that Americans were being swept up in a wave of extraordinary affluence beginning in the 1980s, but rather that one class of Americans was essentially taking its leave of the rest of us. Hourly wages were dropping, the stock market was rising, taxes for the rich were falling, public housing was not a priority anymore, and in-your-face tract mansions were sprouting everywhere.

Today we call those changes inequality, and inequality is, obviously, the point of the McMansion. The suburban ideal of the 1950s, according to *The Organization Man,* was supposed to be "classlessness," but the opposite ideal is the brick-to-the-head message of the dominant suburban form of today. The McMansion exists to separate and then celebrate the people who are wealthier than everybody else; this is the transcendent theme on which its crazy, discordant architectural features come harmoniously together. This form of development wants nothing to do with the superficial community-mindedness of the postwar suburb, and the reason the giant house looks the way it does is to inform you of this. Have the security guard slam the gates, please, and the rest of the world be damned.

Inequality is the point of the McMansion, and the McMansion is also, to a certain degree, the point of inequality; it's the pot of pyrite at the end of the rainbow of mud that we have chosen as a nation to follow. As you enter its soaring narthex of an entrance, keep this in mind: before you, in the skim-coated drywall great room and the monster granite kitchen with its multiplicity of faucets and its Viking stove—this is what it is all about. This is the reward of thirty-odd years of economic policy.

There have always been grand houses in America. What put them into mass production in the mid-1980s? The most obvious answer is that decade's transfer of wealth to professionals and managers, a shift made possible by the top-bracket tax cuts of 1981. Where corporate earnings had previously been spent on skyscrapers and company planes, the money now poured into the personal bank accounts of executives. Tax policy then steered those executives' spending toward residential real estate. As the economist James K. Galbraith reminded me, "The 1986 Tax Reform Act removed the deductibility of non-mortgage interest," leaving mortgage interest as the only remaining deductible type and thus "creating a powerful incentive for households to try to own their own homes."

Signs of what was coming appeared in 1983, when the *New York Times* ran a feature on gated communities—or "cities behind walls"—which the paper depicted as a rare but slightly alarming development. KB Home, a construction company specializing in single-family houses, went public in 1986. It was followed a year later by the Toll Brothers firm, famous today for its mass-produced châteaux.

In 1986 and 1987, the booming luxury home market became a standard media meme; the *Wall Street Journal* ran a story on "megahouses" in Atlanta, while the *Chicago Tribune* marveled at how "attention has shifted from affordable pricing and downsizing to sprawling luxury houses." In another story, the *Trib* marveled to learn that average house prices had topped one million dollars in certain New York suburbs; in a third, it speculated that all this had something to do with the rise of investment banking, because of the " 'new money' being generated" on Wall Street.

A careful tracker of upper-class taste all through the 1980s, the *Tribune* checked off the arrival of such now-standard luxuries as the dual dishwasher, the cathedral ceiling, and, in 1987, the enormous bathroom: "The white-marble whirlpool tub is perched regally on a pedestal at the end of the room below a mirror and a Palladian window. The tub, with gold-plated faucets and onyx handles, is flanked by fluted, decorative columns, suggesting ancient Greece or Rome." It was, the paper suggested, part of a happy trend in which developers were industriously "coming up with new rooms" heretofore not thought to be necessary (or not thought of at all), such as "studios" for children and "game rooms," not to mention the now obligatory "master retreat." All this space creation came with an ideology, too, or a marketing scheme, anyway. "Our homes are a reflection of the achievements, success, affluence and impeccable taste of each of our custom home clients," a suburban Chicago developer told the paper. "We attract those who want more than a place to live; they want a style of living, too."

These weren't machines for living as much as they were machines for flattering. Architecturally speaking, they were straight-up botches. Take a driving tour of the eighties palaces of Potomac, Maryland (an early tract-mansion hot zone), and marvel at the elements of pseudo-classical style: The glorious entrances. The random ornament stapled on here and there. The pointless skinny columns. The helter-skelter proportions. The toaster-shaped windows that would make Palladio want to stick his head in the oven.

The obvious problem for McMansion designers, both then and now, was what to do with the structure's vast exterior walls. In the early days, the facades were often flat and simple and covered with brick veneer, but as the houses grew they evolved the complicated folds and bulges and gables-on-gables-on-gables that are so familiar today. Other notable features were introduced as the years passed: the turrets, the theater rooms, the gift-wrapping rooms, the attached gazebos, those enormous and complicated circus-tent roofs. But all that really matters— in the eighties and today—is the building's size, meaning the square feet enclosed by its particleboard perimeter. A number, by the way, that increases almost every year even as the number of people per household steadily declines.

Living in one of these cavernous châteaux, a friend of mine says, is like being a pea bouncing around in a packing crate. But what one begins to suspect, after looking at enough of them, is that these garish houses aren't designed for living in at all, really; they are designed to sell, and to resell, and to sell yet again. Sometimes, according to a passage in the 2000 book *Suburban Nation,* by Andrés Duany, Elizabeth Plater-Zyberk, and Jeff Speck, the purpose of all this tacky architecture is to create a strong impression on a potential buyer in the first few minutes of a realtor-guided visit. These are assets, not homes. They are built to flip: human settlements organized around the premise of the Greater Fool Theory.

They weren't called McMansions at first, of course; that epithet came later. The man who bears the most responsibility for popularizing the term seems to have been Duany, the well-known architect and proponent of "New Urbanism." A Florida newspaper quoted Duany using the term in 1990, and he could be found using it himself in an article he co-wrote for the *Wilson Quarterly* in 1992. His critique of the McManse—"the fast-food version of the American dream," it segregated people by income and it forced us to drive if we wanted to go anywhere—was part of a lecture he gave criticizing botched planning in the suburbs.

Google the word and you will find that nearly everyone who uses it criticizes McMansions. It is a universally hated architectural form. Indeed, after unemployment and the activities of investment bankers, the McMansion may be the most despised aspect of capitalism there is.

Those who defend suburbia, on the other hand, often do it in the same way people used to defend inequality itself: by invoking the democracy of the market. You might not like tract mansions (or Walmart, or asset bubbles, or daytime television), but the market that created these things is giving the people what they want. These houses are gaudy, in other words, because we want gaudy; they're big because we want big; to criticize them or any other aspect of consumer culture is to imagine yourself smarter or better than the average consumer. (Besides, as certain libertarian thinkers claimed back in the innocent 1990s, the ever increasing size of the American home, plus all those awesome new appliances, were examples of progress.)

The fog of market populism grew particularly thick when issues of suburban development came up. *Edge City*, Joel Garreau's influential 1991 book celebrating malls, developers, tract mansions, and office parks, started with this sentence: "The controversial assumption undergirding this book is that Americans basically are pretty smart cookies who generally know what they're doing." Once upon a time, Garreau reportedly felt threatened by giant suburban homes, but eventually he came to an epiphany. Suburbia is something we Americans built by choice, he realized, as a common democratic project. To sneer at disorderly new developments, as highbrow urban planners do, is an act of disdain.

And, by extension, to deride McMansions can be interpreted as only one thing: an act of snobbery toward the rich.

There's an even stranger way in which the McMansion tracks the larger debate about inequality. Every time the pundit class has convinced itself that the conservative era is ending—that we are about to return to the good old postwar liberal way—it has also declared the end of the tract mansion. Markets crash, unemployment spikes, editorial writers declare that the American people have had it with policies that favor the rich—oh, and that the trend toward ever bigger houses is over.

The first time this happened was in the early 1990s. The economy was in recession and it looked as if the conservative era represented by Ronald Reagan was coming to a close. In his bestselling 1990 book *The Politics of Rich and Poor,* Kevin Phillips declared that inequality had gone so far that it would trigger an inevitable explosion of middle-class rage. The eruption came right on schedule in 1992, when everything was supposed to be about "the economy, stupid" and the superficially populist Democrat Bill Clinton was elected president. At about the same time, the architect Duany was touring the country lecturing about the blight of the gigantic suburban home. A *Washington Post* staff writer, Henry Allen, was describing the McMansion as a stale leftover from the fading days of the Reagan boom.

But nothing really changed, either in politics or in suburban development patterns. The fortunes of the rich continued to soar on Bill Clinton's watch, and the McMansions of the 1990s soon exceeded those of the 1980s in the two essential categories of square feet and contemptuous vulgarity. Eventually, and with the help of further deregulations and Republican tax cuts, the greatest real estate boom of them all got going, driven (as we now know) by colossal chicanery in the mortgage business . . . and the appraisal business . . . and the investment-banking business . . . and the bond-rating business as well.

And so came the inevitable replay, beginning in 2007: economic collapse, anger at bankers, a lot of talk about "hope," a populist political explosion—and a shared judgment that the trend toward ever gaudier houses was over. On the latter subject, at least, it was more than just talk this time around. Wrecked subdivisions and abandoned McMansions blighted the landscape from California to Connecticut after the housing bubble burst; countless pictures remain online to remind us of what this desolation looked like and there are even stock photos available of this quintessential image of the Great Recession. More shockingly, in 2009 the average size of new American houses began to decrease. News stories proclaiming the "Death of the 'McMansion'" proliferated. *Fortune* magazine ran a story about the "New Affordability" in housing.

Again, however, nothing really changed. After a brief experiment with deficit spending, President Obama made his famous turn to austerity. The one percent got the best of both policies: not only were they bailed out, but they also chalked up some of their best years ever under Barack Obama, taking home 95 percent of the nation's income growth during the recovery. Meanwhile, the New Affordability in housing went the way of the short-lived "Keynesian resurgence" in economic policy. In 2011, average square footage in houses resumed its upward swing; in 2012 the *Wall Street Journal* launched a new weekly section called "Mansion"; in 2013 average house sizes surpassed the pre-collapse record set in 2008.

Of course there *was* something different this time around. In the 2008 collapse, the real estate bust wasn't the *result* of some larger economic trend but the *cause* of it. Although we are accustomed to blaming it all on subprime loans, about half of the disaster was actually attributable to the less well-known fiasco in Alt-A instruments, which fed the McMansion market—the "liar's loans" that were securitized and sold off stamped with a big triple-A. The worst recession of our lifetime, in other words, was in large part the result of our superiors' longing to get themselves a piece of the grandiose.

That astounding reversal of the usual chain of cause and effect changed the way I thought about the McMansion. I once thought of writing an essay tracking stylistic changes in the tract-mansion form—how, say, the fake French simplicity of Newt Gingrich's 1987 McMansion gave way to the complex multigabled fakery of Michele Bachmann's 2007 McMansion, with maybe a stop in between to contemplate Ricky Bobby's McMansion in *Talladega Nights.*

But what I discovered is that the form doesn't really change. Yes, the houses get bigger every year, gables and gazebos come and go, but what is really striking about the McMansion is its vapid consistency as the decades pass.

What stays the same, and what always gets me when I walk through one of these houses, are the vacuous spaces. The vast stretches of painted Sheetrock. The gaping rooms that are too tall to decorate. The billowing industrial roof. The windowless walls.

There's something else, too. Stand in the street when the sun hits the McMansion from the right angle and its glare obliterates the fake muntins in the windows, and suddenly you grasp the truth about this form: it is staring at you with those blank featureless eyes, those empty holes in that vast, unadorned wall, demanding to be fed. This house doesn't serve humans; we serve it.

This is not some absurdity at the fringe of our way of life. This is civilization's very center, the only thing that really makes sense in our crazy asphalt tangle, the tawdry telos at which all our economic policies aim. Everything we do seems designed to make this thing possible. Cities must sprawl to accommodate its bulk, eight-lane roads must be constructed, gasoline must be kept cheap, coal must be hauled in from Wyoming on mile-long trains. Your taxes must be higher to make up for the deductions given to McMansion owners, lending standards must be diluted so more suckers can purchase them, banks must be propped up, bonuses must go out, stock prices must ascend. Every one of us must work ever longer hours so that this millionaire's folly can remain viable, can be sold successfully to the next one on the list. This stupendous, staring banality is the final outcome for which we have sacrificed everything else.

(2014)

Home of the Whopper

Let me tell you about this one stretch of Hillsborough Road in Durham, North Carolina. It's between two freeways, just a short drive from the noble towers of Duke University, and in the space of about a mile you will find a McDonald's, a Cracker Barrel, a Wendy's, a Chick-fil-A, an Arby's, a Waffle House, a Bojangles', a Biscuitville, a Subway, a Taco Bell, and a KFC. As you walk down this roaring thoroughfare, you'll notice that the ground is littered with napkins and bright yellow paper cups. But then again, you aren't really supposed to be walking along this portion of Hillsborough Road and noticing things like those cups, or that abandoned concrete pedestal for some vanished logo, or the empty vodka bottle hidden behind that broken Motel 6 sign. This is a landscape meant to be viewed through a windshield and with the stereo turned up. In fact, drivers here sometimes seem bewildered by the very presence of pedestrians, which may be the reason I was almost run down twice.

But it wasn't a car that struck me on Hillsborough Road; it was a vision: a spontaneous understanding of fast-food efficiency. I was gazing on a simple yellow structure that contained the workings of a Waffle House when it came to me—the meaning of this whole panorama of chain restaurants. The modular construction, the application of assembly-line techniques to food service, the twin-basket fryers and bulk condiment dispensers, even the clever plastic lids on the coffee cups, with their fold-back sip tabs: these were all triumphs of human ingenuity. You had to admire them. And yet that intense, concentrated efficiency also demanded a fantastic wastefulness elsewhere—of fuel, of air-conditioning, of land, of landfill. Inside the box was a masterpiece of industrial engineering; outside the box were things and people that existed merely to be used up.

I tried to imagine the great national efforts that had made such lunatic efficiency possible. There were the agricultural subsidies and the irrigation projects and the many highway construction programs, not to mention the mass media, without which our greatest brands could never have been built. Had all these mighty enterprises been undertaken simply to create the amazing but utterly typical landscape of Hillsborough Road? To ensure that certain parties might make tons of money while others made almost nothing at all?

I was in Durham on August 29, 2013, to observe something unusual in this particular industry: a strike. What made it especially unusual is that it was happening in North Carolina, which is both hostile to unions and—as the birthplace of Hardee's, Bojangles', and Krispy Kreme—a kind of fast-food Athens.

The action began at a Burger King, a lonely-looking outpost holding down one corner of a bleak intersection. A handful of workers and their supporters gathered there at six in the morning, forming their line on the sidewalk even before the sun rose. After some preliminary small talk, they stirred themselves into action and began to chant: "Workers' rights are human rights!" Mustering enthusiasm wasn't easy at that hour, however, and the chant didn't take. They tried another, and eventually got themselves pumped up: "We can't survive on seven twenty-five!"

TV news crews soon showed up, as did two police cruisers. A single silhouetted customer sat by the window inside the beleaguered BK and contemplated the scene. As rush hour began, passing drivers honked to show their support.

Later that morning, the protest moved to a McDonald's in downtown Durham, then to a Little Caesars located in a strip mall on a busy eight-lane road in Raleigh. The strikers, whose numbers had grown, stood by the curb and waved their signs at motorists while their children played in the mulch under the tiny suburban trees behind them. Drivers of semitrailer trucks blew their horns in solidarity; drivers of pickup trucks yelled insults.

The last stop of the day was a Raleigh KFC. It was nearly four in the afternoon by then, and it was plenty hot. The protesters, now numbering around 150, had rallied at a nearby Baptist church before heading over to vent their displeasure at the Colonel's jolly empire. And this time they were accompanied by the Reverend William Barber II, leader of North Carolina's

NAACP chapter and the organizer of weekly protests against the far-right state legislature that have led to nearly a thousand arrests.

A big man with a slight arthritic stoop, Barber worked the crowd in a resonant bass voice. Standing on the lawn in front of the KFC, he sketched out the moral framework of the protest— that no matter how many hours fast-food employees work, they'll never get anywhere at minimum wage. What they wanted, Barber declared, was the right to enjoy "the fruit of their own labor," a line he quoted from the state's Reconstruction-era constitution. And then he lowered the boom. "I stopped by to tell you that the fruit is spoiled. The fruit is *spoiled* when you can work in Kentucky Fried Chicken and can't hardly buy the chicken that's there. The fruit is *spoiled* when you can work and feed other people and can't hardly feed your own children."

It was a day of revolt against the batter-fried god Efficiency and his eleven esoteric herbs and spices, and an air of jubilation hovered over the protesters as they made their way down Tarboro Street back to the church. Residents of the tiny houses along the route stood in their doorways and cheered as the workers passed. And the strikers themselves, back in the church parking lot and filled with the joy of collective action, began to dance.

There have been countless news stories on the national wave of fast-food strikes, but what I saw that day in North Carolina wasn't exactly a strike in the traditional sense of the word. In several other cities, cashiers and fry cooks walked off the job in sufficient numbers to close restaurants down. That didn't happen in Raleigh-Durham. What I saw was more protest than work stoppage, and the most visible organization at the rallies was not a union but a community-organizing outfit called Action NC. Very few people, if any, were actually skipping their shifts. Not surprisingly, then, the workers I met seemed a little unfamiliar with the customary rules of labor agitation. One protester wore a stylish black dress and high heels—as she told me, she hadn't anticipated how physically demanding picketing could be. The protesters made little effort to dissuade customers from entering the restaurants, and as the day got hotter some went inside themselves to order cold drinks. Several of the people I interviewed also seemed to assume that they needn't fear retaliation by management. These were all innocent mistakes, of course—and the kind of confusion you would expect to see in the least unionized state in the Union.

Their grievances, however, were the real thing. Willietta Dukes, dressed in dark clothes and with a crucifix on a cord around her neck, told me about her job at a local burger franchise. She is, to judge by her story, an employee who cares about the restaurant, about keeping it shipshape and getting to know regular customers. But after working for various fast-food franchises for sixteen years and raising two children on minimal pay, she's now living in her grown son's spare room and barely staying afloat.

By contrast, Dukes says, managers boast about the bonuses they receive, and one has even shared a favorite stress-reduction technique: every day he goes home and climbs into his hot tub. "I don't even *have* a home to go to!" Dukes tells me. And though her employers are tightfisted with wages, Dukes says she received a form letter warning her about the dangers of labor unions— sent via FedEx.

Lucia Garcia, who had brought her cheerful six-year-old son to the picket line, told me about working at a suburban McDonald's, where she has the relative good luck to be paid $7.95 per hour, seventy cents above the minimum wage. But despite this munificence, and the fact that her husband works as well, she and her family have been forced to rely on church food pantries to get by, an ironic state of affairs for someone who works in food service, and an emotionally difficult one as well. "It's sad for me," Garcia said, "because sometimes it embarrasses my girls."

Everyone knows how poorly fast-food jobs pay. They also know why this is supposed to be okay: fast-food workers are teenagers, they don't have kids or college degrees, and it's an entry-level job. Hell, it's virtually a form of national service, the economic boot camp that has replaced the two years our fathers had to give to the armed forces.

Every one of these soothing shibboleths was contradicted by what I saw in North Carolina. These days, fast-food workers are often adults, they often do have children, and I met at least one college grad among the protesters in Raleigh. Why are things like this? Because a job is a job, and in times as lean as ours, the Golden Arches may be the only game in town, regardless of qualifications and degrees.

What people who repeat the shibboleths also don't know is how much effort has gone into keeping fast-food pay so low, despite the enormous profits raked in by the chains. In fact, the conditions of employment have been engineered almost as carefully as the brands and the burgers—engineered to achieve the complete interchangeability of workers.

In his classic *Fast Food Nation* (2001), Eric Schlosser describes the industry's manic pursuit of standardization. The food arrives at the restaurant mostly frozen; the machines that do the cooking are foolproof; virtually no skills are required. "Jobs that have been 'de-skilled' can be filled cheaply," writes Schlosser. "The need to retain any individual worker is greatly reduced by the ease with which he or she can be replaced." Indeed, these are not really restaurants at all but "food systems," a term favored by the companies themselves. And naturally these systematizers are militantly anti-union. Schlosser tells of a "flying squad" of McDonald's executives who roamed the country during the 1960s and 1970s, stamping out pro-labor sentiment. The National Restaurant Association, for its part, was a leading opponent of the federal "card check" legislation in 2009, which would have made it easier to form unions, and the industry also supports such private-sector propagandists as Rick Berman, a gifted translator of biz-think into the common sense of the millions.

By and large, Americans love the men who systematized their food. Our culture is awash with celebrations of the heroes who plucked pearls of efficiency from the grease traps of the nation. Think: the brave entrepreneurs who pioneered the fifteen-cent hamburger. The brave entrepreneurs who gave the fifteen-cent hamburger people a little competition. The brave entrepreneurs who brought fake Mexican food to the heartland, or who figured out a quicker way to bake a pizza or fluff a biscuit or "build" a submarine sandwich. They publish their memoirs. They are the heroes of Hollywood movies. They are saluted by presidential candidates. They run for president themselves.

And then there is the army of slightly less heroic entrepreneurs known as franchisees, the people who harness their ambition to a brand and a food system developed by someone else. They may not be Wilber Hardee or Harland Sanders, but they are still risk-taking individualists, tirelessly pushing some kettle corn concept or dedicating their lives to the advancement of Hawaiian-style smoothies. We love them, too. They are our "neighbors," as an angry commentator on Fox News put it during a segment on the fast-food strike; they are people, said another, who "worked their rear ends off all their life, put up their own risk capital."

These myths are powerful stuff. They were reiterated in 2012 by the Republican presidential candidate, Mitt Romney, who extolled the "entrepreneurial spirit" of Jim Liautaud, the founder of Jimmy John's Gourmet Sandwiches. People like Liautaud "don't look to governments," Romney insisted, in a campaign speech in suburban Chicago. "They instead look to themselves and say: What can I do to make myself better? What things can I do to enhance the prospects for myself and my family?"

But while these practitioners of self-improvement through food systems may not "look to governments," government sure does look out for them. I refer not only to roads and sewers and small-business loans but also to something much more direct. As I discovered in North Carolina, many if not most fast-food workers receive food stamps or some other form of government assistance. When they say, "We can't survive on seven twenty-five!" they mean it quite literally—they can't survive on the minimum wage, and neither can you, if you are trying to "enhance the prospects" of your family by feeding them.* So government steps in and graciously makes up the difference with our tax dollars, thereby excusing management from paying workers enough to keep them and their families, you know, alive.

"It's an honest living," Willietta Dukes told me the day of the action in North Carolina, by way of explaining why she should be paid more. "I'm a hard worker."

These were direct statements, made without guile. But despite the legend of the scrappy fast-food entrepreneur, I wonder how many chain-store bosses can truthfully say they make an "honest living." The managers at the restaurants in Raleigh-Durham declined to talk to me, so it's difficult to form any judgment about them as individuals. The fast-food companies themselves, however, are well-known entities. Vast corporations making vast profits, they deal in often unhealthful food and pay their leading executives princely sums. And increasingly they are the property of the same hardworking bankers who brought you the economic slump that never ends.

Consider Burger King, which (let the shameful record show) I once preferred to certain other ubiquitous burger joints. Today the chain is little more than a shuttlecock for private equity. Acquired in 1997 by Diageo, the liquor multinational, it was sold in 2002 to a consortium of financial institutions—including, of course, Goldman Sachs and Bain Capital—which took the company public in 2006. It was next acquired by the Brazilian-backed investment firm 3G Capital, which took it public again

---

* Congress has not voted to raise the federal minimum wage since 2007. Although Barack Obama called for an increase many times, he was not able to persuade Congress to act on the matter.

in 2012 and merged it with Tim Horton's, the Canadian dough-nut chain. Along the way, Burger King fumbled its position as the number two American burger chain.

Similar stories are everywhere you care to look. Bojangles', the fried-chicken chain, used to be owned by Falfurrias Capital Partners, which eventually off-loaded it to a private equity firm called Advent International; the chain then went public in 2015. Sun Capital Partners owns Friendly's, Johnny Rockets, and Boston Market. Fog Cutter Capital Group owns Fatburger. Consumer Capital Partners owns Smashburger. And then there is Roark Capital—yes, named after Ayn Rand's individualist architect—which owns Arby's, Cinnabon, Carvel, Seattle's Best Coffee, Moe's Southwest Grill, and (perhaps tellingly) a trash col-lection company called Central Jersey Waste and Recycling.

Even the franchisees, the moms and pops who run your beloved local chain restaurant, aren't that mom-and-poppy any-more. Here, too, the Wall Street folks have seen a good thing—a reliable source of revenue made possible by rock-bottom wages. The largest Burger King franchisee, for example, is a publicly traded company in Syracuse, New York, that runs some 762 local restaurants; its CEO took home $2.4 million in 2016, counting stock awards. Another big BK operator was once Strategic Restaurants, which is owned by Cerberus Capital. The largest tranche of Pizza Hut franchises is owned by something called Olympus Growth Fund V, which bought it in 2011 from Merrill Lynch Global Private Equity. And let us not overlook the doughty folks at Valor Equity, which owns a string of Little Caesars and Dunkin' Donuts locations through its Utah subsid-iary Sizzling Platter.

At both the corporate and the franchise levels, industry officials were keeping their mouths shut about the strike, and for obvious reasons. Acknowledging worker discontent is a no-win situation for enterprises that have invested so much in depicting themselves as enclaves of family-friendly happiness. I mean, nothing deflates a carefully constructed brand image like an angry worker standing out front screaming about not being able to vaccinate her six-month-old on said brand's lousy pay.

However, the industry's D.C. attack dog, the aforementioned Rick Berman, felt no such compunction and commenced snarling immediately. On the day of the strike in August 2013, his Employment Policies Institute ran a full-page advertisement in the *Wall Street Journal* featuring a big photo of a Japanese kitchen robot. The fast-food protests "aren't a battle against management," the ad proclaimed, but a "battle against technology." Should workers push too hard for super-size wages, shiny automatons might well be deployed in restaurants across the country, making you-know-who totally redundant.

The implication of this message was that companies employ humans as an act of charity. If those ingrate humans mouth off too much, our noble companies will just go ahead and take the bottom-line steps they've magnanimously refrained from taking until now. "Hard work" and an "honest living" actually mean nothing in this world; capital means everything. Look on my technology, ye powerless, and despair!

I thought about that nightmare of automation for quite a while after Berman's ad ran. It has a grain of truth to it, of course. Journalists have been replaced with bloggers and crowd-sourcing. Factory hands have been replaced with robots. University professors are being replaced with adjuncts and MOOCs. What else might the god Efficiency choose to de-skill?

Here's a suggestion: how about the ideological carnival barkers in D.C.? The fast-food strike triggered a predictable pundit reaction, and as I watched the creaking libertarian apparatus send its suit-and-tie spokesmen before the cameras to denounce unions, I wondered how long capital would stand to be represented in this old-fashioned way. In many cases, the kind of people I'm describing haven't had an original thought in years. Their main job is to appear concerned on Fox News and collect a six-figure sinecure at some industry-subsidized think tank. To say that they "work hard" for an "honest living" would be to bend meaning to the point where its fragile chicken bones snap beneath its rubbery flesh. In a sane world, they are the ones who would be most profitably replaced, their corner of the CNBC screen filled instead by Hatsune Miku–style projections, attractive Republican holograms whose free-market patter could be easily cued up by a back-office worker in Bangalore.

Boddie-Noell Enterprises is one of the great fast-food success stories in North Carolina. It was among the first to open a franchise of Hardee's, a restaurant selling cheap hamburgers after the McDonald's model, and over the years Boddie-Noell grew to become the biggest Hardee's franchisee of them all. The company has not been purchased by some faceless private equity firm, and it is not the sort of outfit that would ever run advertisements threatening to replace its workers with robots.

On the contrary, it is a family-owned business whose slogan is "We Believe in People." Boddie-Noell feels such concern for its people that the company claims to have a phalanx of

"Corporate Chaplains" on call, ready to "offer care to employees with personal and professional life issues."

Boddie-Noell Enterprises also owns a plantation. In saying this, I am not making a snarky comment about the conditions of fast-food employment. I mean a *real* plantation outside Nashville, North Carolina, named Rose Hill. Its main house was completed in the 1790s by the ancestors of the Boddie family, and its ups and downs over the decades roughly parallel the vicissitudes of American capitalism itself.

The Boddies lost Rose Hill in the depths of the Depression but were able to buy it back in 1979, as their archipelago of cheap hamburger stands grew. Yes, their antebellum paradise was regained through the miraculous intercession of fast-food efficiency, and now the family has converted Rose Hill into a conference center and a favorite venue for elegant plantation-style weddings.

The day after the strike, I drove out to Rose Hill. It was indeed impressive. I approached the plantation by an allée of crape myrtle trees in full flower, and passed through an imposing brick-and-iron gateway bearing the Boddie coat of arms (which does not feature a hamburger couchant on a field of honey-mustard dipping sauce). I drove on, was waved at by a man mowing a lawn, and finally reached the main building, where I had the beautifully landscaped parking area all to myself.

The manor house certainly looked authentic—white and stately, the ceiling of the grand, four-columned front porch painted exactly the right shade of blue. I rang the doorbell: nothing. I gazed out over the attractive swimming pool: nobody. With the exception of the man on the mower, Rose Hill seemed completely depopulated.

I have no doubt that this place swarms with people when conferences are in session or weddings in progress. But seeing it empty in this way triggered another epiphany, a vision of a world in which workers and their troubles had completely disappeared. Yes, they will persist as smiling faces in company newsletters. Yet the day will come when technology and ideology make them absolutely interchangeable, each bearing a silver tray loaded with deep-fried hors d'oeuvres: a support staff for the entrepreneurial schemes and romantic fantasies of the ones who can still afford individuality.

(2013)

Meet the DYKWIAs

Let us turn now to the airport, the civic trophy through which so many of us will pass over the next few months. Despite its function, the airport is not a utilitarian but rather a utopian structure, designed (at the high end, anyway) with architectural aspirations that fall somewhere between a world's fair pavilion and Chartres cathedral.

Like those structures, the airport is designed to instruct us in the goodness of our social order. Of course, that order changes from time to time. When it was under construction in the 1930s, Washington's National Airport was referred to as the "people's airport," with all the social-democratic connotations one might expect. The landmark structures of air travel's postwar period were monuments to The Future, with soaring roofs, or wings like an enormous bird, or a great circular crown apparently designed to accommodate flying saucers. Unfortunately, that golden future was indefinitely postponed as the airline industry adopted super-sized airplanes, security checkpoints, and an ever growing number of passengers and flights.

The utopian impulse is still with us, however; it has merely moved indoors. Think of the grand open spaces of the modern airport, with its sweeping curves and colored surfaces and its walls of light and glass.

The subject of the structure's optimism has changed as well. Airports are no longer shrines to the majesty of the common man, or even to the magnificence of the future. What today's airport instructs us in are the wonders of globalization. It is a museum of sacred corporate art. From the CNBC-sponsored bookstores selling volumes on innovation and leadership to the advertisements that decorate the walls of every concourse, what the passenger absorbs as he walks through this stately space are lessons in the glory and the soulfulness of market-based civilization.

The advertisements I am describing are not really for products per se, although airports have plenty of those, too. What interests me are the solemn philosophical declarations made by godlike corporate beings: announcements of high-minded public concern, noble promises made to a suffering world. "We added technology to strategy," intone airport ads for the Accenture consultancy. "You get the multiplier effect." There are small children whose mouths hang open at the "brighter world" promised by the Dutch conglomerate DSM, makers of plastics and food additives. United Technologies tells us how "revolutionary" they are and also how "green" and "empowering," which are damned fine things to be.

My personal favorite is the series of ads with which IBM once covered the entire length of a big boarding area at what is now called Reagan National Airport. None of them promoted items that IBM actually sold, but rather Progress itself, what the company called a "smarter planet." Each of them made me want to raise my voice in song. "Now every doctor knows you personally," declared one of them. "Food is now followed from farm to fork," announced another. And then, on into the realm of the cyber-miraculous: "Drivers now see traffic jams before they happen." "Now more suitcases find their way home." And—praise the Lord—"Any child can access a first-class education." Right down to the mundane, wonders abound in this world that IBM hath made: "Shirts can pick a tie for you."

The solemn nobility of the business traveler is another common theme in the airport shrine. Ads depict her toiling heroically from unusual locations, thanks to her native industriousness and a little assist from a smartphone or an understanding hotel chain. The airlines themselves are particularly assiduous flatterers of this key demographic, forever reminding the business traveler that the place he has entered is a magical realm of high-tech ease and deep concern for his every need; that each treasured business traveler is in fact a member of a prestigious association of accomplished professionals, a person of elite status. Excuse me, a person of *premier sapphire elite medallion* status, maybe even a person so exalted that his status must be kept secret from the world. Oh, and how much savvier is he than the clueless folk who travel but once or twice a year and clutter up the boarding area like a herd of cattle.

What's more, the airport informs the business traveler, his accomplishments are so magnificent that he deserves to board ahead of others, to sit in special seats, to turn the concierge key and step into the glistening premises of a special secret lounge. The flattery doesn't stop in the terminal, either, but continues on in the majestic images the airlines make you watch while sitting in the plane, along with the soaring, slowed-down Gershwin music, all of it attesting to how very awesome it all is, and how very much they care.

It would be easy to overlook all this stuff, because we have all been told for years that the airport is the center of the globalized World That Is to Come, and so its transformation into a propaganda experience for big biz is something we sort of expect. It would be easy to overlook, that is, if not for the fact that the airport experience is *the opposite of utopian.*

Often it is sordid. Sometimes it is downright awful. You have to hustle because you're running late. The flight is delayed. It costs twenty minutes and twenty-five dollars to check a bag. Your shoes have to come off. The electrical outlets have all been claimed, and by people who appear to have been lying on the floor for quite some time. There's a long line at the gate. No room in the overhead compartments. The plane smells of soiled diapers. Your seat turns out to have been designed to accommodate a child and, just for good measure, an argument ensues over whether you may recline it. Why would anyone want to claim this experience by plastering it with ads for their management consultancy? Worse: to claim it by enumerating how they've made modern life *wonderful*?

It is truly strange when you stop to think about it, a complete mismatch between advertisement and reality. It's like the 1930s photo of flood victims standing in a line before a billboard declaring, "There's no way like the American way." It's like seeing a commercial for handguns while watching *Dora the Explorer.*

And that's just the perspective from where I sit in K class. Now consider the people who actually work in this environment. Do they feel like joining in the airport's hymn to the business system? Well, there are the flight attendants, whose job was once thought to be glamorous but who are in fact notoriously overworked and who took a huge hit to their pensions in the big airline restructuring after 9/11.

Matters worsen as you descend from there, taking into account the people who handle the baggage, who help with the wheelchairs, and who clean up the bathrooms. Years ago, according to a report issued by the Berkeley Labor Center, such work often paid a middle-class salary; today, thanks to outsourcing and other ingenious techniques of wage suppression, the people who toil at these occupations can expect to spend their lives in a condition of near poverty. There is a reason that residents of SeaTac, Washington, the municipality that surrounds Seattle's Sea-Tac airport and its many first-class lounges, voted to raise the minimum wage to $15 per hour—and there's a reason the entity leading the opposition to them was Alaska Airlines.

I suspect that no one really believes the airport's propaganda, not even the regular business travelers at whom it is aimed. Some of the most caustic and insulting tales you read on frequent-flier discussion boards concern the snobs at the top of the airport's great chain of being—the dopes who believe the hype and really think they are members of a privileged class because they've got a card named for a precious stone.

Usually these stories start with something going wrong, with some privileged someone being made to wait or stand in a line usually designated for the rank and file. His every premier-platinum expectation has been aroused and then thwarted, and he proceeds to take out his impotent frustration on a flight attendant or the person who scans passes at the gate. Eventually, the legend goes, he will fall back on the phrase that seems to be written in the very DNA of every legislative assistant and senior vice president in the land: *"Do you know who I am?"*

Yes, he is a DYKWIA, the ultimate target of the veteran traveler's contempt, and what the DYKWIA shows us is that the whole airport status system is an illusion. I don't think there are really all that many poor folk among the scorned of coach class—with ticket prices what they are these days, those people are driving or taking the bus to their destination. I suspect there aren't that many true one percenters among the airlines' elite programs, either—those people are taking private jets. The prestige the platinum passenger enjoys is merely that of a conscientious consumer, a champion collector of Green Stamps, a hamster who has really made that ol' wheel spin. The life of the real elite goes on somewhere else.

In truth, almost no one here knows who you are, and even fewer care. You may be an emerald coronet five-million-miler—and still you have to let some guy from the TSA go through your luggage in the middle of a glorified shopping mall. When you stop to think about it, the architectural pretentiousness of that glorified mall only amplifies the feeling of frustration and alienation: trying to board an overcrowded bus outside a space-age folly that would be more appropriate in Vegas; queuing up in the freezing cold on the curb of a building by Eero Saarinen; finding almost no amenities flight-side in a brutalist marvel designed in the days before terrorism; looking for a place to rest in a long line of chairs, each one staring at the wall in an endless, windowless hallway that turns out to be in the wrong concourse altogether.

Real luxury is having nothing to do with this at all.

(2014)

Dead End on Shakin' Street

My hometown is vibrant. Its status is certified. It is official. It is stamped on both sides.

There was a time, though, when it wasn't, when my friends and I would laugh at Kansas City's blandness: its harmless theater productions, its pretentious suburbs, its private country clubs, its eternal taste for classic rock. We called it Cupcake Land, after a favorite Richard Rhodes essay from the 1980s. The city knew nothing of the bold ideas of our robust generation, we thought: it had no real, gritty music subculture; it was deaf to irony; hell, it actually tried to drive out of business the last surviving club from its Jazz Age glory days.

Maybe that was the sort of criticism everybody made of their midwestern hometowns back then. Well, those hometowns have certainly turned the tables on us scoffers. Our enthusiasm for music is a dead thing now in these post-alternative decades, a mere record collection that we occasionally cue up after one scotch too many, to help us remember the time when art seemed to matter.

But Kansas City doesn't need any reminders. The place fairly quivers with vitality today. It is swarming with artists; its traffic islands are bedecked with the colorful products of their studios. It boasts a spectacular new performing arts center designed by one of those spectacular new celebrity architects. It even has an indie-rock festival to call its own. And while much of the city's flowering has been organic and spontaneous, other parts of its renaissance were actually engineered by the very class of civic leaders people like me used to deride for their impotence and cluelessness. At that Kansas City indie-rock festival, for example, the mayor himself made a presentation a few years ago, as did numerous local professionals and business leaders.

Besides, as everyone knows, cupcakes are cool nowadays, like yoga or something—the consummate expression of the baker's artisanal vibrancy.

Your hometown is probably vibrant, too. Every city is either vibrant these days or working on a plan to attain vibrancy soon. The reason is simple: a city isn't successful—isn't even a city, really—unless it can lay claim to being "vibrant." Vibrancy is so universally desirable, so totemic in its powers, that even though we aren't sure what the word means, we know that the quality it designates must be cultivated. The vibrant, we believe, is what makes certain cities flourish. The absence of vibrancy, by contrast, is what allows the diseases of depopulation and blight to set in.

This formulation sounded ridiculous to me when I first encountered it. Whatever the word meant, "vibrancy" was surely an outcome of civic prosperity, not its cause. Putting it the other way round was like reasoning that, since sidewalks get wet when it rains, we can encourage rainfall by wetting the sidewalks.

But to others, the vibrancy mantra is profoundly persuasive. The pursuit of the vibrant seems to be the universal job description of the nation's city planners nowadays. It was also part of the Obama administration's economic recovery strategy for the nation. In the fall of 2011, the National Endowment for the Arts launched "ArtPlace," a joint project with the nation's largest banks and foundations, and ArtPlace immediately began generating a cloud of glowing euphemisms around the central, hallowed cliché.

> ArtPlace is investing in art and culture at the heart of a portfolio of integrated strategies that can drive vibrancy and diversity so powerful that it transforms communities.

Specifically, the way vibrancy was supposed to transform communities was by making them more prosperous. ArtPlace used to say its goal was not merely to promote the arts but to "transform economic development in America," a project that was straightforward and obvious if you accepted the organization's slogan: "Art creates vibrancy and increases economic opportunity."

And that, presumably, is why everyone is so damn vibrant these days. Consider Akron, Ohio, which in 2012 was the subject of a conference bearing the thrilling name "Greater Akron: This Is What Vibrant Looks Like." Or Boise, Idaho, whose citizens, according to the city's Department of Arts and History, were "fortunate to live in a vibrant community in which creativity flourishes in every season." Or Cincinnati, which is the home of a nonprofit called Go Vibrant as well as of the Greater Cincinnati Foundation, which used to hand out "Cultural Vibrancy" grants, guided by the knowledge that "Cultural Vibrancy is vital to a thriving community."

Is Rockford, Illinois, vibrant? Oh, my God, yes: according to a local news outlet, the city's "Mayor's Arts Award nominees make Rockford vibrant." The Quad Cities? Check: as their tourism website explains, the four hamlets are "a vibrant community of cities sharing the Mississippi River in both Iowa and Illinois." Pittsburgh, Pennsylvania? Need you even ask? Pittsburgh is a sort of Paris of the vibrant; a city where dance parties and rock concerts enjoy the vigorous boosting of an outfit called Vibrant Pittsburgh; a place that draws young people from across the nation to frolic in its "numerous hip and vibrant neighborhoods," according to a blog maintained by a consortium of Pittsburgh business organizations.

Then there are the unfortunate places from which the big V is said to have receded, like the "once-vibrant" Cincinnati/Northern Kentucky International Airport, where remediation efforts are thankfully under way. Detroit has for years provided the nation's opining class with sobering lessons on what happens when the vibrant evaporates, and the fear that such a fate might befall other scenes and other communities still occasionally makes headlines. According to the *Hartford Courant,* a looming "shortage of vibrancy" gave the Connecticut business community quite a scare in 2007, while the city fathers of Cleveland took a peep at all that was vibrating in Seattle back in 2002 and suspected that they were losing the race: "Without that vibrancy, Cleveland may decline."

The real Sahara of the vibrant, though, is that part of America where lonely midwestern farmers live among what the *New York Times* calls "crumbling reminders of more vibrant days." This is a land from which vibrancy has withdrawn its blessings; the disastrous depopulation that has followed is, according to vibrancy theory, the unavoidable consequence. In small towns, bored teen-agers turn their eyes longingly to the exciting doings in the big cities; they pine for urban amenities such as hipster bars and farmers' markets and indie-rock festivals. Like everyone else, they want the vibrant and they will not be denied.

As with other clichés, to describe a city as vibrant was once a fairly innovative thing to do. Before 1950, the adjective was used mainly to describe colors and sound—the latter of which, after all, is transmitted through the air as vibrations. People's voices were often said to be vibrant. As were, say, notes played on an oboe. To apply the adjective to a "community" or a "scene," on the other hand, was extremely unusual back then. In fact, the word "vibrant" does not seem to appear at all in Jane Jacobs's 1961 urban classic *The Death and Life of Great American Cities*, even though that book is often remembered as the manifesto of vibrancy theory. How the expression made the leap from nov-elty to gold-plated bureaucratic buzzword is anyone's guess.

The real force behind our mania for the vibrant is the nation's charitable foundations. For organized philanthropy, "vibrant" seems to have become the one-stop solution for all that ails the American polis. A decade ago there were other obsessions: multiculturalism, or public-private partnerships, or leadership programs. But now, it's *"Get southern Illinois some vibrancy and its troubles are over."*

"A vibrant arts community strengthens our region," the website of the Seattle Foundation used to declare, describing art as a way of attracting and retaining awesome corporate employers. The New England Foundation for the Arts spends its substance "to nurture a vibrant ecology for dance." The Kresge Foundation "seek[s] to build strong, vibrant communities—enlivened by the presence of healthy cultural organizations and well-resourced artists." The S. D. Bechtel, Jr. Foundation says it's "dedicated to advancing a productive, vibrant, and sustainable California." The Greater Tacoma Community Foundation hands out "Vibrant Community" grants to local nonprofits, while the "Vibrant Communities" program of Montreal's J. W. McConnell Family Foundation seems to be a sort of antipoverty initiative.

But while everyone agrees that "vibrancy" is the ultimate desideratum of urban life, no one seems to be exactly sure what vibrancy is. In 2012, the Municipal Art Society of New York held a panel discussion—excuse me, a "convening"—of foundation people to talk about "Measuring Vibrancy" (it seems "the impact of arts and cultural investments on neighborhoods . . . is hard to quantify"). In retrospect, it would have been far better to convene such a gathering before all those foundation people persuaded the cities of the nation to blow millions setting up gallery districts and street fairs.

Even ArtPlace, the big vibrancy project of the NEA, the banks, and the foundations, was not entirely sure that vibrancy could be observed or quantified. That's why the group worked to develop what it called Vibrancy Indicators: "While we are not able to measure vibrancy directly," the group's website admits, "we believe that the measures we are assembling, taken together, will provide useful insights into the nature and location of especially vibrant places within cities."

What are those measures? Eventually, ArtPlace would settle on ten categories that were pretty much exactly what you would expect ("Creative Industry Jobs," for example, and "Cell Phone Activity"). Even before these were announced, however, the organization had published a presentation on the subject that included this helpful directive: "Inform leaders of the connection between vibrancy and prosperity."

So vibrancy brings prosperity, which we know because prosperous places are vibrant ones. Got that? Read enough of this material and it starts to feel as if nothing can deter the committed friend of the vibrant: if you know it's the great good thing, you simply push ahead, moving all before you with your millions.

This is not the place to try to gauge the enormous, unaccountable power that foundations wield over American life—their agenda-setting clout in urban planning debates, for example, or the influence they hold over cash-strapped universities, or their symbiosis with public broadcasters NPR and PBS.

My target here is not their power but their vacuity. The members of our leadership class look out over the trashed and looted landscape of the American city, and they solemnly declare that salvation lies in an almost meaningless buzzword—that if we chant that buzzword loud enough and often enough, our troubles are over.

Back in the day, my friends and I at the *Baffler* loved to mock, analyze, and deride money's cultivation of the cool. Just think of all the permutations of urban hipness that have flickered by since we first undertook that mission: Rollerblading near water.

"Potemkin bohemias" like Chicago's Wicker Park. Richard Florida's "creative class." And while each of these fads came and went, here is what also happened: utilities were privatized to disastrous effect, the real estate bubble grew and burst, the banks got ever bigger, state governments declared war on public workers, and the economy went off a cliff.

It is time to acknowledge the truth: that our leaders have nothing to say, really, about any of this. They have nothing to suggest, really, to Cairo, Illinois, or St. Joseph, Missouri. They have no comment to make, really, about the depopulation of the countryside or the deindustrialization of the Midwest. They have nothing to offer, really, but the same suggestions as before, gussied up with a new set of clichés. They have no idea what to do for places or people that aren't already successful or that have no prospect of ever becoming cool.

And so the dull bureaucrat lusts passionately for the lifestyle of the creative artist, but beneath it all is the harsh fact that foundations have been selling the vibrant, under one label or another, for decades; all they've done this time is repackage it as a sort of prosperity gospel for Ivy League art students. As the name of a suburban St. Louis street festival puts it, without the smallest detectable trace of irony, "Let them eat art."

In the face of this deafening silence, allow me to propose a working hypothesis of what makes up the vibrant. It is a quality you find in cities or neighborhoods where there is an arts or music "scene," lots of restaurants and food markets of a certain highbrow type, trophy architecture to memorialize the scene's otherwise transient life, and an audience of prosperous people who are interested in all these things.

Art production is supposed to be linked, through the black

box of "vibrancy," to prosperity itself. This is something so obvious that just about everyone concerned agrees on it. "Corporations see a vibrant cultural landscape as a magnet for talent," goes the thinking behind Kansas City's vibrancy, according to one report; it's "almost as vital for drawing good workers as more-traditional benefits like retirement plans and health insurance." (In other words, art is literally a substitute for compensating people properly. "Let them eat art," indeed.) And so when the Cincinnati foundation known as ArtsWave informs the world that "the arts create vibrant neighborhoods and contribute to a thriving economy," it is voicing a sentiment so commonplace in foundation-land that it is almost not worth remarking on.*

How does art do these amazing things? you might ask. Reasoning backward from the ultimate object of all contemporary civic planning—attracting and retaining top talent, of course—the ArtPlace website pronounced thus:

> The ability to attract and retain talent depends, in part, on quality of place. And the best proxy for quality of place is vibrancy.

Others have spelled out the formula in more detail. We build prosperity by mobilizing art people as vibrancy shock troops and counting on them to . . . well . . . *gentrify* formerly

---

* This organization used to be some dreadful highbrow outfit called the Fine Arts Fund, until the day in 2010 when it turned on and got hip and figured out that its mission should be "to advance the vitality and vibrancy of Greater Cincinnati by mobilizing the creative energy of the entire community." Behold: ArtsWave was born.

bedraggled parts of town. Once that mission is accomplished, then other vibrancy multipliers kick in. The presence of hipsters is said to be inspirational to businesses; their doings make cities attractive to the class of professionals that everyone wants; their colorful japes help companies to hire quality employees; and so on. All a city really needs to prosper is a group of art-school grads, some lofts for them to live in, and a couple of thrift stores to supply them with the ironic clothes they crave. Then we just step back and watch them work their magic.

In this respect, we are counting on our artists for considerably more than we did during the country's previous experience with economic breakdown, but also—in other respects—considerably less.

In the thirties, the federal government launched a number of programs directly subsidizing artists. Painters got jobs making murals for the walls of post offices and public buildings; theater troupes staged plays; writers collected folklore; photographers combed the South documenting the lives of sharecroppers. But no one expected those artists to pull us out of the Depression by some occult process of entrepreneurship kindling. Instead, government supported them mainly because they were unemployed. In other words, government then did precisely the opposite of what government does today: in the thirties, we protected artists from the market, while today we thrust them out into it, imagining them as the stokers on the hurtling job-creation locomotive.

Both then and now, we heard much about "scenes." The public art of the thirties was, famously, concerned with "the American scene," via the style known as regionalism. Thomas Hart Benton painted Missouri scenes, John Steuart Curry painted

Kansas scenes, and unemployed writers assembled tour guides to every state in the Union.

In today's more vibrant version, though, the artist himself is the spectacle, the subject of the tour guide. His primary job is not necessarily to produce art but to participate in a "scene"—in an act that is put on for well-heeled spectators. Indeed, this act is essential to the vibrant: in order to bring the economic effects that "the arts" are being counted upon to bring—the attraction and retention of top talent for a city's corporations, remember—the artist himself must be highly visible. He must run a gallery, patronize cool coffee shops and restaurants, or rehab run-down buildings.

The imagined audience is also different. "Art for the millions" was the slogan in the 1930s, and federal programs then aimed to improve both cities and rural settlements, to make them more livable for everyone. Today, however, we have a different public in mind. Vibrancy is a performance that artists or musicians are expected to put on, either directly or indirectly, for the corporate class. These are the ones we aim to reassure of our city's vibrancy, so that they never choose to move their millions (of dollars) to some more vibrant burg. An artist who keeps to herself, who works in her room all day, who wears unremarkable clothes and goes without tattoos—by definition she brings almost nothing to this project, adds little to the economic prospects of a given area. She inspires no one. She offers no lessons in creativity. She is not vibrant.

The public art of the thirties was often heavy-handed, close to propaganda even, but it was also intensely concerned with the lives of ordinary people. The vibrant, on the other hand, would separate the artist from such boring souls. The creative ones are to be corralled into a "scene" where they work their magic, pumping up real estate prices and inspiring creative-class onlookers. But what of the people no one is interested in attracting and retaining? Millions of Americans go through their lives in places that aren't vibrant, in areas that don't have a "scene," in jobs that aren't rewarding, in industries that aren't creative; their experiences are, almost by definition, off-limits for artistic contemplation.

Instead of all that, the aesthetic of the vibrant proposes a tail-chasing reverence for creativity itself, a power that is supposed to inspire the businessperson-spectator and lead him or her to conjure up bold and outside-the-box thoughts. Consider the trophy buildings that are, inevitably, the greatest expression of vibrancy theory—the assorted Frank Gehry and pseudo-Gehry structures that every city council seems to believe it must build as a sort of welcome mat to the creative class. Regardless of the particular shape that each structure's fluttering and swooping exterior takes, the point of the buildings is, in a general sense, to flaunt their eccentricity, to conspicuously defy the straight lines and cheap construction materials of the conventional buildings that surround them.

There is, of course, an obvious contradiction here. On the one hand, vibrancy theory treats the artist as a glorified social worker, whose role is to please children and stimulate businessmen and support the community. But the means by which the community is to be supported is always some species of vanguardism or conspicuous creativity. The whole point of the vibrant is to build prosperous economies, to help business succeed; and yet prosperous business communities, with their Babbitt-like complacency and their air-conditioned cubicles and their office-park buildings, are precisely what we expect artists to flout and defy.

A second problem: Why is it any better to pander to the "creative class" than it is to pander to business in the usual way? One strategy uses "incentives" and tax cuts to get companies to move from one state to another, while the other advises us to emphasize music festivals and art galleries when we make our appeal to that exalted cohort. But neither approach imagines a future arising from something other than government abasing itself before the wealthy.

Let's say that the foundations successfully persuade Akron to enter into a vibrancy arms race with Indianapolis. Let's say both cities blow millions on building cool neighborhoods and encouraging private art galleries. But let's say Akron wins. Somehow its planned vibrancy catches on and, thanks to a particularly piquant whirligig installation, it is able to steal away Indianapolis's businesses. Akron "attracts and retains"; it becomes a creative-class hot spot. It leaves Indianapolis an empty hulk on the prairie.

What then? Is the nation better served now that those businesses are located in Akron rather than in Indianapolis? Or would it have been more productive to spend those millions on bridges, railroads, highways, or even to hire a thousand angry bloggers to demand better bank regulation?

It really doesn't take a whole lot of "creativity" to come up with real answers to our big problems. You just need to change the questions slightly. How about, instead of serving some targeted fraction of the master class, we choose to give an entirely different group of Americans what they wanted? Even if those Americans weren't cool? What would that look like?

A while ago I was talking about rural depopulation with an officer of a Kansas farmers' organization; as it happened, he had thought about the problem a great deal. Using arts festivals to make small towns appear "vibrant"—a favorite stratagem of ArtPlace—was not one of his suggestions. What he proposed instead was universal health coverage.

Other solutions to the problem of rural depopulation are just as easy to come up with. Prohibit corporate agriculture; this would encourage not only small farms but food diversity as well. Use zoning rules to restrict big-box stores, thereby saving small-town merchants. Make college excellent and affordable, so that graduates aren't forced by the weight of student debt to seek corporate employment in the big cities. Resist the urgings of foundation dignitaries and focus instead on the far less beguiling reverie of durable, productive enterprise.

For any of this to happen, though, the vibrancy Ponzi scheme first has to bottom out; the creative class must face its final Götterdämmerung. So hop to it, Akron: convert your very last rubber factory to an artist's loft, bring on the indie-rock festivals, and borrow millions in order to get a sweeping new titanium city hall designed by Rem Koolhaas. Go vibrant—and go for broke.

(2012)

PART 2

TOO SMART TO FAIL

Academy Fight Song

We begin with utopia—the utopia known as the American university system. It is the finest educational institution in the world, everyone tells us. Indeed, to judge by the praise that is heaped upon it, the American university may be our best institution, period. With its peaceful quadrangles and prosperity-bringing innovation, the university is more satisfying than the church, more nurturing than the family, more productive than any industry.

What universities produce are dreams. Like other utopias—like Walt Disney World, like the ambrosial lands shown in perfume advertisements, like the competitive Valhalla of the Olympics—the university is a place of wish fulfillment and infinite possibility. It is the four-year luxury cruise that will transport us gently across the gulf of class. It is the wrought-iron gateway to the land of lifelong affluence.

It is not the university itself that tells us these things; it is *everyone* that does. It is the president of the United States. It is our most respected political commentators and economists. It is our business heroes and our sports heroes. It is our favorite teacher and our guidance counselor and maybe even our own Tiger Mom. They've been to the university, after all. They know.

When we reach the end of high school, we approach the next life, the university life, in the manner of children writing letters to Santa. We promise to be so very good. We open our hearts to the beloved institution. We get good grades. We do our best on standardized tests. We earnestly list our first, second, third choices. We tell them what we want to be when we grow up. We confide our wishes. We stare at the stock photos of smiling students, we visit the campus, and we find, always, that it is so very beautiful.

And when that fat acceptance letter comes—oh, it is the greatest moment of personal vindication most of us have experienced. Our hard work has paid off. We have been chosen.

Then several years pass, and one day we wake up to discover there is no Santa Claus. Somehow, we have been had. We are a hundred thousand dollars in debt, and there is no clear way to escape it. We have no prospects to speak of. And if those damn dreams of ours happened to have taken a particularly fantastic turn and urged us to get a Ph.D., then the learning really begins.

Go back to the beginning, back to the days when people first understood a character-building college education to be the ticket to middle-class success. We were going to forge a model republic of citizen-students, who would redeem the merit badges of academic achievement for spots in the upper reaches of corporate capitalism. The totems of the modern American striver were to be the university credential and the corner office, and prosperity would reward the ablest.

And so the story remains today, despite everything that has happened in the realms of the corporation and the university. We might worry from time to time about the liberal professors who infest the academy, but higher learning is still where you go to "write your destiny," to use President Obama's 2010 description of education generally. Go to college, or else your destiny will be written by someone else. The bachelor's degree that universities issue is a "credential" that's "a prerequisite for 21st century jobs," the White House website used to say. Obama himself equated this credential with upward mobility—more schooling equals more success—as well as with national greatness. "The kinds of opportunities that are open to you will be determined by how far you go in school," he once declared.

> In other words, the farther you go in school, the farther you'll go in life. And at a time when other countries are competing with us like never before; when students around the world are working harder than ever, and doing better than ever; your success in school will also help determine America's success in the 21st century.

The words are eloquent, but the sentiment is unremarkable. Everyone says this. It is obvious. Thomas Friedman, the *New York Times* foreign affairs columnist who has refashioned himself into the Lord Protector of Learning in recent years, says the same thing, constantly: you'd better have the schooling and the

skills that employers demand if you want to make even a minimal living. The higher education mantra is possibly the greatest cliché in American public life.

And so the dreams proliferate. Education is the competitive
advantage that might save our skins as we compete more and
more directly with China and Vietnam and the Philippines, the
journalists say. Education is what explains income inequality,
chime the economists, and more education is what will roll it
back. In fact, education is just about the only way we can justify being paid for our work at all; it is the only quantifiable
input that makes us valuable or gives us "skills."

Quantifiable, yes, but only vaguely. No one really knows the
exact educational recipe that is supposed to save us. It is, again,
a dream, a secret formula, a black box into which we pour money
and out of which comes uplift and enrichment and wish fulfillment. How a college education manages to do these marvelous
things—Is it calculus? Is it classics?—is a subject of hot controversy. All we know for sure is that people who go to college are
affluent; it follows naturally that if you send more people to college, you will have yourself a more affluent country.

It's simple, really. Get yourself a bachelor's degree from a
"good school" and those dreamy dreams of yours can come true.
Get something else, like a cosmetologist's license or a member-
ship in the International Brotherhood of Teamsters, and you lose.

What everyone agrees on is this: higher education is the
industry that sells tickets to the affluent life. In fact, they are
the only ones licensed to do this. Yes, there are many colleges
one can choose from—public, private, and for-profit—but col-
lectively they control the one credential that we believe to be of
value. Everything about them advertises it. The armorial logos,

the Gothic towers, even the names of the great colleges, so red-
olent of money and privilege and aristocracy: Duke and Princeton
and Vanderbilt. If you want to succeed, you must go to them;
they are the ones controlling the gate.

What they sell, in other words, is something we believe to
be so valuable it is almost impossible to measure. Anyone in her
right mind would pay an enormous price for it.

Another fact: this same industry, despite its legal status as a
public charity, is today driven by motives almost indistinguish-
able from those of the profit-maximizing entities traded on the
New York Stock Exchange.

The coming of "academic capitalism" has been anticipated
and praised for years; today it is here. Colleges and universities
clamor greedily for pharmaceutical patents and ownership
chunks of high-tech start-ups; they boast of being "entrepreneurial"; they have rationalized and outsourced countless aspects of
their operations in the search for cash; they fight their workers
nearly as ferociously as a nineteenth-century railroad baron; and
the richest among them have turned their endowments into in-
house hedge funds.

Now, consider the seventeen-year-old customer against whom
this predatory institution squares off. He comes loping to the
bargaining table armed with about the same amount of guile
that, a few years earlier, he brought to Santa's lap in the happy
holiday shopping center. You can be sure that he knows all about
the imperative of achieving his dreams, and the status that will
surely flow from attending a "good school." Either he goes to college like the rest of his friends or he goes to work.

He knows enough about the world to predict the kind of
work he'll get with only a high school diploma in his pocket,

but of the ways of the university he knows precious little. He is the opposite of a savvy consumer. And yet here he comes nevertheless, armed with the ability to pay virtually any price his dream school demands that he pay. All he needs to do is sign a student loan application, binding himself forever and inescapably with a financial instrument he only dimly understands and that, thanks to the optimism of adolescence, he has not yet learned to fear.

The disaster that the university has proceeded to inflict on the youth of America, I submit, is the direct and inescapable outcome of this grim equation. Yes, in certain reaches of the system the variables are different and the yield isn't quite as dreadful as in others. But by and large, once all the factors I have described were in place, it was a matter of simple math. Grant to an industry control over access to the good things in life; insist that it transform itself into a throat-cutting, market-minded mercenary; get thought leaders to declare it the answer to every problem—and, last, send it your unsuspecting kids, armed with a blank check drawn on their own future.

Was it not inevitable? Put these pieces together, and *of course* attendance costs will ascend at a head-swimming clip, reaching $70,000 a year now at some private schools. *Of course* young people will be saddled with life-crushing amounts of debt; *of course* the university will use its knowledge of them—their list of college choices, their campus visits, their hopes for the future—to extract every last possible dollar from the teenage mark and her family. It is lambs trotting blithely to the slaughter. It is the utterly predictable fruits of our simultaneous love affairs with college and the market. It is the same lesson taught us by so many other disastrous privatizations: in our passion for entrepreneurship and meritocracy, we forgot that maybe the market wasn't the solution to all things.

An educational publisher wrote to me in 2013; it wanted to reprint an essay of mine that had been on the Internet, where it is available for free. The textbook in which it wanted to include it, the publisher said, would be "inexpensively priced," and authors were therefore being asked to keep their reprint fees to a minimum. The low, low price that students were to pay for this textbook: $75.95. "Approximately."

I was astounded, but it took just a few minutes of research to realize that $76 was, in fact, altruistic by the standards of this industry. Paying $250 for a textbook is more like it nowadays; according to one economist, textbook prices have increased *812 percent* over the last thirty-odd years, outstripping not only inflation (by a mile) but every other commodity—home prices, health care—that we usually consider to be spiraling out of control.

The explanation is simple. The textbook publishers use every trick known to the marketing mind to obsolete their products year after year, thus closing off the possibility of secondhand sales. What's more, textbook publishing is a highly concentrated industry—an oligopoly—which means that publishers can drive prices pretty much as high as they feel like driving them. Meanwhile, the professors who assign the textbooks and who might do something about the problem don't have to pay for them.

Actually, that explanation isn't simple *enough*. The truth is that rip-offs like this abound in academia—that virtually every aspect of the higher-ed dream has been colonized by monopolies, cartels, and other predators—that the charmingly naive American student is in fact a cash cow and everyone has got a scheme for slicing off a porterhouse or two.

Consider the standardized-testing industry and its shadow the test-prep industry. One of them is supposedly charitable, the other ebulliently profit-minded, but both of them have raked it in for years by stoking a pointless arms race among the anxious youngsters of the nation, each kid fearful lest their dream be canceled out by someone else's. The testing companies, each of which holds a monopoly over some aspect of the business, charge students hefty registration fees, pay their executives fantastic salaries,* and scheme endlessly to enlarge the empire of the standardized test—persuading more people to take advanced placement exams, for example, and invading grade schools, where "No Child Left Behind" and the push for a "Common Core" have opened up vast frontiers for testing.

The test-prep people, meanwhile, match them step for step, charging students hefty fees to help them beat the standardized tests and trying to persuade new demographics—grade-schoolers, notably—that they need cram school, too. Occasionally news stories appear announcing that test prep of this kind has little effect on SAT scores, but it's really the news stories themselves that have little effect. What parent is going to be stingy when their child's future appears to be at stake? And so the test-prep industry has boomed extravagantly for decades now; there are

---

* Fantastic, that is, by the standards of public charities. The testing companies clearly see themselves as participants in the larger world of business and pay their executives accordingly. This is why the president of the College Board received "compensation" to the tune of $1.3 million in 2009.

numerous entrants in the field, and the most established of them, Kaplan Inc., has branched out around the globe and into all manner of educational provinces.*

And we're not even going to start with the test-*fraud* industry, which is apparently booming as well, as cases of mass cheating surface at Harvard, at New York City's prestigious Stuyvesant High, at the benchmark-crazy Atlanta Public Schools, and in South Korea, where SATs for the whole country had to be canceled in 2013.

Consider the "enrollment management" industry, which helps colleges and universities acquire the student body they desire. Since what this means in many cases is *students who can pay*— the opposite of the "inclusiveness" most universities say they treasure—enrollment management is a job best left to quiet consultancies, who use the various tools of marketing to discover a student's "price sensitivity." In other words, if you give a discount of a certain amount to a student with a certain SAT score, will that be enough to persuade them to pick up the rest of the tab and attend your school? What will it take to lure them to their second choice? Their third? Enrollment management consultants know the answer, just as they know what discounts

---

* "It takes the concept all the way to zero years old!" Jonathan Grayer told *Forbes* in 2000. Grayer was then the CEO of Kaplan, the well-known test-prep company; he was speaking to *Forbes* about Kaplan's acquisition of a company that aimed to improve the math and reading abilities of kids in elementary school. *Forbes* continued: "In the case of a very young child, he explains, the parent who buys the book *Curious George* could be supported online with tutorial help: Instead of just reading the book to little Caitlin, a tutor might suggest the parent ask, 'What did Curious George learn from his experience with the broken bicycle?' "

to offer in order to maximize the institution's revenue and boost its all-important rankings.

Consider the sweetheart deals that are so commonplace between university administrations and the businessmen who happen to sit on the university's board of directors. Consider universities' real estate operations, which are often thuggish and nearly always tax-free. Consider their army of Washington lobbyists, angling for earmarks and fighting accountability measures. Consider their offshore financial holdings. Or their sleazy arrangements with tobacco companies and Big Pharma and high-tech start-ups.

And last, consider the many universities that have raised their tuition to extravagant levels for no reason at all except to take advantage of the quaint American folk belief that price tags indicate quality. From this faith in price correctness the nation apparently cannot be moved—there is simply no amount of exposure or reporting that will do it—and so the university inevitably becomes a luxury good, like a big Armani label you get to wear through life that costs a fortune but that holds little intrinsic worth at all. "It serves as a trophy, a symbol," the former president of George Washington University told *Washington Monthly* magazine in 2010, describing his own (successful) strategy for making GWU into a top-tier school via gigantic tuition hikes. "It's a sort of token of who they think they are."

It is all so wonderfully circular, is it not? We know college degrees make us affluent because affluent people have college degrees; we also know that we must spend lots of money on college—signing up for a life of debt, essentially—because we believe status signifiers like college ought to be fantastically expensive. Think about it this way for long enough and you start to suspect that maybe those fancy stickers you put in your rear window are what education is all about, the distilled essence of the whole thing.

A particularly poignant educational scandal of recent years had to do with Cooper Union, the prestigious Manhattan art and architecture school, which, from its founding in 1859 up till 2014, offered an excellent education for free to everyone who was admitted. The way it did this was by carefully living on the limited funds generated by its endowment. Suddenly this could no longer be sustained, and the school announced that it would begin charging students $20,000 for tuition. The reason everything had to change was that Cooper Union, like . . . well, like every other institution of higher ed in America, decided a few years back that it needed to think big and embrace change and build the brand. First step in that process: erecting a fantastically expensive bit of trophy architecture across the street from its main building. (There was also a growing corps of administrators, and a departing president who needed to be paid close to $1.1 million, but we won't go into that now.) Unfortunately, Cooper Union couldn't pay for this glamorous new tower, and so it had to borrow an enormous sum, as other corporations do. The "free education" thing was collateral damage. Better to be known for "vibrant" architecture, I guess, than for some old-fashioned nonsense about uplifting the nonwealthy.

The story of Cooper Union is a typical anecdote of the age of collegiate capitalism, and it's easy to come up with other examples of the lavish, unnecessary spending that characterizes American academia nowadays that makes it "the best in the world." It's not just the showy new buildings, but the sports teams that give the alumni such a thrill, the fancy gymnasiums and elaborate food courts that everyone thinks you have to have if you want the cool kids to choose your school over the others. It's the celebrity professors everyone has decided they must furnish sinecures for regardless of whether those celebrities know anything about the subject they are hired to profess.

Above all, what the masters of academia spend the loot on is themselves. In saying this, I am not referring merely to the increasing number of university presidents who take home annual "compensation" north of a million dollars. That is a waste, of course, an outrageous bit of money burning borrowed from Wall Street in an age when we ought to be doing the opposite of borrowing from Wall Street. But what has really fueled students' ever growing indebtedness, as anyone with a connection to academia can tell you, is the insane proliferation of university administrators.

The political scientist Benjamin Ginsberg tells the sorry tale in his 2011 book *The Fall of the Faculty.* Back in the day, Ginsberg tells us, American universities were governed by professors, who would take time out from their academic careers to manage the institution's business affairs. Today, however, the business side of the university has been captured by a class of professionals who have nothing to do with the pedagogical enterprise itself.

Administrators: their salaries are generous, their ranks expand year after year, and their work requires no peer review and not even much effort. As Ginsberg reminds us, most of them don't teach courses, they don't squabble like English professors at the MLA, and no one ever suggests replacing them with adjuncts or temps. As tuition balloons, it is administrators who prosper. In fact, their fortunes are an almost exact reverse image of the tuition-indebtedness of the young.

According to Ginsberg, "administrators and staffers actually outnumber full-time faculty members" nowadays, even though it's the faculty members who do the real work of education. The numbers are startling. While the ranks of full-time professors have grown at about the rate of university enrollment generally since 1975—which is to say, about 50 percent—administrations have expanded at an amazing pace. The number of administrators proper is up 85 percent, Ginsberg reports, while the number of "other professionals" employed by universities has grown 240 percent. Their share of university budgets has grown by similar margins.

Naturally, an ugly new class conflict has begun to play out amidst the leafy groves. Administrators, it seems, have understood that the fortunes of their cohort are directly opposed to those of the faculty. One group's well-being comes at the expense of the other, and vice versa. And so, according to Ginsberg, the administrators work constantly to expand their own numbers, to replace professors with adjuncts, to subject professors to petty humiliations, to interfere in faculty hiring.

It is not until you read Ginsberg's description of the day-to-day activities of administrators that the lightbulb goes on, however. The particular pedagogy that motivates this class of university creatures is . . . management theory. They talk endlessly about "process management" and "excellence." They set up "culture teams." They attend retreats where they play team-building games. And whole divisions of them are dedicated to writing "strategic plans" for their university, which take years to finish and are forgotten immediately upon completion.

The attempted coup at the University of Virginia in 2012 gave us a glimpse of how this conflict can play out. The university's president at the time was a sociologist, a traditional academic; the university's Board of Visitors was dominated by wealthy figures from finance and real estate who wanted (of course) to dump the classics department and who thought the university needed to get with the online thing toot sweet because David Brooks had said it was a good idea in his *New York Times* column. When the board members forced the president to resign, they cloaked the putsch in a stinky fog of management bullshit.

At first, the only explanation available for the ouster came in a leaked email from a super-wealthy trustee of the business school—Mr. Jefferson's university suffered from a troubling paucity of "strategic dynamism," he moaned. Oh, but that would change now that the moneymen were in charge: "There will also be a strategic planning initiative commenced by the Board of Visitors with a focus on strategic dynamism." Billionaire alumnus Paul Tudor Jones II soon chimed in with a newspaper op-ed informing Virginians that Jefferson himself would have welcomed the coup because he was a "change agent." Reading these preposterous declarations at the time, I was convinced there had to be some deeper motive, that no one really talked this way. Since then, however, we've learned that these people *meant this stuff.* Read the board members' emails back and forth to one another and you start to realize that the poor president was the casualty of a long-running argument the university brass had been having among themselves about . . . "the rate of change."*

That the people who hold the ultimate authority at our institutions of higher learning are dedicated to a notorious form of pseudo-knowledge is richly ironic, and it is also telling. The point of management theory, after all, is to establish the legitimacy of a social order and a social class who are, in fact, little more than drones. The grotesque top heaviness of the American corporation is an old story: we have more supervisors per worker than any other industrialized nation, and quite naturally we have developed an extensive literature of bogus social theory assuring those supervisors of the rightfulness of their place in the world—a literature that also counsels everyone else to accept their subordinate station in the Great Chain of Free-Market Being.

The deprofessionalization of the faculty is another long-running tragedy that gets a little sadder every year, as teaching college students steadily becomes an occupation for people with no tenure, no benefits, and no job security. These lumpen-profs, who have spent many years earning advanced degrees but sometimes make less than minimum wage, now account for more than three quarters of the teaching that is done at our insanely expensive, oh-so-excellent American universities. Their numbers increase constantly as universities continue to produce far more Ph.D.s

---

* The emails were obtained with a FOIA request by the University of Virginia student newspaper, the *Cavalier Daily*.

than they do full-time, tenure-track job openings, and every time cutbacks are necessary—which is to say, all the time—it is those same full-time, tenure-track job openings that get pruned.

What can I add to this dreadful tale? That it continues to get worse, decades after it began? Is there anything new to be said about the humiliation that the lumpen-profs suffer at the hands of their so-called colleagues? Can I shock anyone by describing the shabby, desperate lives they lead as they chase their own higher-ed dream? Will it do any good to remind readers how the tenured English dons of thirty years ago helped to set the forces of destruction in motion simply because producing more Ph.D.s meant a lighter workload for themselves?

No. What matters now is that the deed has been done. We have all seen how it went down and which disciplines have fared the worst—as it happens, the very disciplines that, back in the 1980s, housed the most fashionable, the most respected, the most theoretically advanced, the most *intimidating* people on campus. Their heirs have been transformed into minimum-wage flunkies. They were once the consummate academic players, and look at them now.

What their downfall shows us is just how easily systems of this kind can be made to crumble. There is zero solidarity in a meritocracy, even a fake one, as the writer Sarah Kendzior showed in a series of hard-hitting articles on the adjunct situation. Just about everyone in academia believes that they were the smartest kid in their class, the one with the good grades and the awesome test scores. They believe, by definition, that they are where they are because they deserve it. They're the best. So tenured faculty find it easy to dismiss the deprofessionalization of their field as the whining of second-raters who can't make the grade. Too many of the adjuncts themselves, meanwhile, find it difficult to blame the system as they apply fruitlessly for another tenure-track position or race across town to their second or third teaching job: maybe they just don't have what it takes after all. Then again, they will all be together, assuredly, as they sink finally into the briny deep.

The system can't go on this way. It is too obviously a rip-off, on too many levels, with too many victims. One of these days a breaking point will come, just as it did with Enron and the dotcoms and the housing bubble, and all the fine words spoken by our thought leaders will once again be recalled to make them look like imbeciles.

It's easy to understand what *ought* to be done about the higher-ed situation; there is a huge literature on this subject. The scandal has been understood, to varying degrees, for decades. Every example I have used here, every argument I have made, has been made or used by someone else already; after all, the people who have seen this go down are people who can write. The country was up in arms about tuition inflation in the 1980s. Bill Readings published his depressing prediction, *The University in Ruins,* back in 1996. The *Wall Street Journal* ran a shocking page-one story on enrollment management that same year. The proletarianization of the Ph.D. has been the subject of countless exposés since the days of a teaching-assistant strike at Yale in the mid-nineties; I own two books of essays on the subject and no doubt there are a dozen more. Chris Newfield's account of managerialism and higher ed appeared in 2003, and Jennifer

Washburn's *University, Inc.* in 2005. Stanley Aronowitz predicted the slow demise of the professoriate in 1997, and Frank Donoghue told us exactly how the end was coming in *The Last Professors,* published in 2008.

What *ought* to happen is that everything I've described so far should be put in reverse. College should become free or very cheap. It should be heavily subsidized by the states, and robust competition from excellent state U's should in turn bring down the price of college across the board. Pointless money drains such as a vast administration, a preening president, and a quasi-professional football team should all be plugged up. Accrediting agencies should come down like a hammer on universities that use too many adjuncts and part-time teachers. Student loan debt should be universally refinanced to carry little or no interest and should be dischargeable in bankruptcy, like any other form of debt.

But repeating this feels a little like repeating that it will be bad if newspapers go out of business en masse. Of course it will. Everyone knows this. But knowing it and saying it add up to very little.

Despite the academy's noisy radicalism, its endangered meritocracy simply cannot summon the will to challenge the market tide. And virtually no one in politics has proposed taking the obvious steps that are needed to solve the problem.

What actually *will* happen to higher ed, when the breaking point comes, is an extension of what has already happened, what money wants to see happen. Another market-driven disaster will be understood as a disaster of socialism, requiring an ever deeper penetration of the university by market rationality. Trustees and presidents will redouble their efforts to achieve some ineffable "excellence" they associate with tech and architecture and corporate sponsorships. There will be more standardized tests and more desperate test prep. The curriculum will be brought into a tighter orbit around the needs of business, just as Thomas Friedman wants it to be. Professors will continue to plummet in status and power, replaced by adjuncts in ever more situations. An all-celebrity system, made possible by online courses or some other scheme, will finally bring about a mass faculty extinction—a cataclysm that will miraculously spare university administrations. And a quality education in the humanities will once again become a rich kid's prerogative.

And so we end with dystopia, with a race to the free-market bottom. What makes it a tragedy is that President Obama was right when he would talk about education's importance. Not because college augments our future earning power, or helps us compete with Bangladesh, but because the pursuit of knowledge is valuable in its own right. This is why every democratic movement from the Civil War to the 1960s aimed to bring higher ed to an ever widening circle, to make it more affordable. Ours is the generation that stood by gawking while a handful of parasites and billionaires smashed it for their own benefit.

The only way out is for students themselves to interrupt the cycle. Maybe we should demand the nationalization of a handful of struggling universities, putting them on the opposite of a market-based footing, just as public ownership reformed the utilities in the previous century. Maybe the college-aged should forgo the annual rituals and turn their eyes to German or Argentine universities, in the same way that their grandparents use

Canadian pharmaceuticals to hitchhike on a welfare state that hasn't yet been completely compromised. Maybe it's time for another free speech movement, a nationwide student strike for tuition reform and debt relief. Whatever we do, it's time to wake up from the dream.

(2013)

A Matter of Degrees

In March 2012, two hundred thousand protesters took to the streets of Montreal, clashing with police and triggering the Quebec legislature's passage of Bill 78, which placed strict limitations on Canada's traditional freedom of assembly. What motivated this demonstration, among the biggest acts of civil disobedience in Canadian history? Financial malfeasance? Another war in Iraq? No and no. What brought the vast throng to the barricades was a proposed increase in Quebec's college tuition rate, from an annual average of about $2,100 to $3,700.

Americans could only observe this spectacle with bewilderment. For decades, we have sat by placidly while the average price of college has grown astronomically.

Then again, Americans know something about higher education that Canadians don't: the purpose of college isn't education, per se. According to a 2011 article in the *Review of Economics and Statistics,* American undergrads spend less time at their studies nowadays than ever. At the most reputable schools, meanwhile, they get great grades no matter how they perform.

But we aren't concerned about any of that. Americans have figured out that universities exist in order to open the gates of social class, and we pay our princely tuition rates in order to obtain just one thing: the degree, the golden ticket, the capital-C Credential.

The question that naturally follows is: given the rigged nature of the higher-ed game, why would self-interested actors continue to play by the rules? The answer, to a surprising extent, is that they don't.

It is a simple thing to pop a "von" into your name and pass as faded Austrian aristocracy. It doesn't cost much to get one of those Bluetooth earpieces and walk around with it clipped to your head all day like important people used to do. It is also easy to fake a college degree—indeed, there is an entire industry out there ready to help you do it.

We know how easy it is because people are caught doing it all the time, usually after a long career in which the forged Credential attracted no notice. In May 2012, the CEO of Yahoo! quit when it was discovered that his degree in computer science was bogus. In 2006, the CEO of RadioShack stepped down amid a similar scandal—he had exaggerated his accomplishments at a California Bible college. And in 2002, the CEO of Bausch + Lomb admitted that the MBA attributed to him in a corporate press release was nonexistent.

There are examples from government, like the high-ranking

former official in the Department of Homeland Security who loved to make her underlings address her as "Doctor," in recognition of the advanced degree she had acquired from a prominent diploma mill. Her exposure led to a 2004 study by the General Accounting Office that scoured federal agencies for the alumni of just three diploma mills—three out of the hundreds of unaccredited Web-based enterprises that will issue you a degree in recognition of what they call life experience. The GAO caught 463 offenders, more than half of them in the Defense Department.

One might assume that academia is practiced at sniffing out counterfeit degrees. But if anything, prestigious universities seem even more prone to dupery than other institutions. In April 2012, the vice dean of the University of Pennsylvania's Graduate School of Education was forced out after it was revealed that he had never earned the Ph.D. listed on his résumé. In 2011, two top officials at Bishop State Community College in Alabama also turned out to have dubious doctorates. In 2010, a senior vice president at Texas A&M lost his job for faking both a master's and a doctorate. (He also garnished his CV with a fiction about having been a Navy SEAL.) And in what may be the most satisfying irony to come our way in many years, the dean of admissions at the Massachusetts Institute of Technology—the very person responsible for assessing academic credentials and, in fact, the author of a book of advice for college-bound students—confessed in 2007 that each of her advanced degrees was strictly imaginary.*

---

* And don't get me started on the matter of fake academic journals, which will not only publish your scholarly work for a nominal sum but also make you an editor.

"The world is awash with fake degrees," says Les Rosen of Employment Screening Resources, a leading background-check outfit. In several of the examples cited above, the fakers actually studied at the institutions named on their résumés—they just failed to graduate. Others conjured their accomplishments out of thin air. Still others simply purchased their Credentials from unaccredited institutions. All three approaches are undoubtedly on the rise. For many years a consultancy in Wisconsin maintained a tally of educational whoppers told by the various job applicants it was asked to investigate; the resulting "Liars Index" (a term the consultancy trademarked) reached its highest level ever in the second half of 2011 before falling off slightly in the following years.

Just how widespread is the problem? Rosen estimates that some 40 percent of job applicants misrepresent in some way their educational attainments. And he reminds me that this figure includes only those people "who are so brazen about it that they've signed a release and authorization for a background check." Among those who aren't checked—who work for companies that don't hire a professional background screener, or who refuse to sign a release—the fudging is sure to be even more common.

In view of the potential rewards to be gained, the prospective faker is well advised to avoid outright lies. The more rational choice may be a diploma mill, an educational institution that exists only on paper, that usually has a prestigious-sounding name, and that simply prints up and sells its credentials. These institutions, which seem to be everywhere, are difficult to track. Sources suggest, however, that diploma mills generate revenues of as much as a billion dollars per year. In a book published in 2012, a former FBI agent estimated that there were more fake Ph.D.s issued in the United States than there are real ones.*

Visit the websites of these spectral institutions and you find that they are dedicated believers in the entrepreneurial view of higher ed. The point of learning is to climb the ladder, period. "Students graduating with degrees open many more doors in their career paths than those with only high school educations," announced the now vanished website of one of the most notorious diploma mills. "Every additional degree earned assures the recipient a lifetime return on their investment," the website of something called Amh*u*rst University used to remind the aspiring applicant, who was offered an extraordinary range of vocational degrees, from "Acquisition Management" to "Quality Assurance."

The graduates or, rather, the customers of such institutions can sometimes be found congregating on networking sites, where they may comment on the soft stupidity of traditional-college grads and on the utility of their own degrees as they climb the ladder of success. Some of them, of course, wax bitter about the humiliation they felt when they were told their degrees were worthless. But these remorseful buyers should take heart: the fake-degree biz has set up numerous fake accreditation agencies to attest to its genuineness.

---

* In 2015, the *New York Times* exposed a vast network of fake schools selling bogus credentials via 370 authentic-looking websites, all of them linked to one of the biggest software companies in Pakistan. Later on, the U.S. Department of Justice estimated that the company reaped some $140 million through its sale of fake degrees.

It takes only a few hours researching these subjects to make you start to wonder about the swirling tides of fraud that advance and retreat beneath society's placid, meritocratic surface. Eventually you start wondering about that surface, too, where everything seems to be in its place and everyone has the salary he or she deserves.

The diploma mills hold up a mirror to the self-satisfied world of white-collar achievement, and what you see there isn't pretty. Think about it this way: who purchases bogus degrees? Many of the customers, of course, are simply people who want to go to college and are taken in by the scam. Many others, judging by how the industry advertises itself, are desperate people whose careers are going nowhere. They know they need a diploma to succeed, but they can hardly afford to borrow fifty grand and waste four years of their lives at Frisbee State; they've got jobs, dammit, and families, and car payments to make. Someone offers them a college degree in recognition of their actual experience— and not only does it sound attractive, it sounds fair. Who is to say that they are less deserving of life's good things than someone whose parents paid for him to goof off at a glorified country club two decades ago? And who, really, is to say that they know less than the graduate turned out last month by some adjunct-run, beer-soaked, grade-inflated but fully accredited debt factory in New England?

Meanwhile, a parallel industry has sprung up to police the boundaries of educational legitimacy, and it, too, has been growing explosively of late, with new and ever more efficient ways of checking an applicant's collegiate record. And as we might expect, the industry has demonstrated its intellectual seriousness by starting a trade group, the National Association of Professional

Background Screeners, to prevent just anyone from claiming to be a background checker. The NAPBS has lobbyists, conferences, best practices, and even seminars on topics like the Fair Credit Reporting Act.

Perhaps the single most spectacular case of résumé fraud to make headlines in recent years was that of Adam Wheeler, a young man who first cheated his way into Harvard as a transfer student, then cheated his way straight to the top of its internal meritocracy, winning honor after honor with fake transcripts, fake grades, and plagiarized essays.

Like the story of the diploma mills, Wheeler's tale has a peculiar, funhouse-mirror relationship to the conventional annals of American achievement. What he produced was a parody of East Coast striving. In his application to Harvard, he claimed to have taken sixteen Advanced Placement tests; to have gone to Andover rather than to the middling public high school he actually attended; to have briefly attended MIT; to be public-minded and community-conscious in every imaginable way.

And that was only the start. Having crashed the gates of the temple in Cambridge, Wheeler later sent out résumés asserting that he had coauthored books with his professors, that he spoke classical Armenian, and that he had written a scholarly study on "maps of ideology." Such preposterous claims were closer to satire than to fraud. Yet Wheeler was able to fool one of the world's most exalted citadels of higher learning by feeding it back mangled bits of its own jargon. Of course Harvard didn't catch on—it just kept showering the con boy with awards and scholarships.

After Wheeler was exposed, Harvard threw the book at him. The brand had to be protected—just think of the people who had paid all that money for a Harvard degree. And so Wheeler was prosecuted for identity fraud and larceny, ordered to repay the $45,806 in scholarships and financial aid he had won, and sentenced to two and a half years in jail. His sentence was initially suspended—but in late 2011, Wheeler was reportedly behind bars again, having violated his probation by listing Harvard on his résumé. That's what you get, I suppose, when you fool Harvard.

When Harvard fools you, a different set of incentives applies. As Jim Newell points out in a 2012 essay about Wheeler, the school's legitimate graduates and grandees—the very cream of the meritocracy crop—count among their number many of the folks who engineered the subprime disaster and the bank bailouts that haunt our economy still. They haven't paid for those crimes of misrepresentation and fraud, nor will they ever.

Never has the nation's system for choosing its leaders seemed more worthless. Our ruling class, flashing its legitimacy at every turn, steers us into disaster after disaster, cheering for ruinous wars, getting bamboozled by Enron and Madoff, missing equity bubbles and real estate bubbles and commodity bubbles. But accountability, it seems, is something that applies only to the people at the bottom, the ones who took out the bad mortgages or lied on their pitiful résumés.

I don't defend fraudsters, of course. But as we wring our hands over the low-level cheaters who get jobs with mail-order degrees, it is important to remember that the pillars propping up our legitimate system are also corrupt: that the sacred Credential signifies less and less each year, even as it costs more and more to obtain. Yet we act as though it represents everything. It's a million-dollar coin made of pot metal—of course it attracts counterfeiters. And of course its value must be defended by an ever expanding industry of résumé checkers and diploma-mill hunters. The boundaries are artificial, and that is precisely why they must be regulated so intensely: they are the only thing keeping the bunglers and knaves who rule us in their jobs.

(2012)

Course Corrections

To the long list of American institutions that have withered since the dawn of the 1980s—journalism, organized labor, mainline Protestantism, small-town merchants—it may be time to add another: college-level humanities. Those ancient pillars of civilization are under assault these days, with bulldozers advancing from two different directions.

On the one hand, students are migrating away from traditional college subjects like history and philosophy. After hitting a postwar high in the mid-1960s, enrollments in the humanities have dropped off sharply, and still show no signs of recovering. This is supposedly happening because recent college grads who chose to major in old-school subjects have experienced more difficulty finding jobs. Indeed, the folly of studying, say, English lit has become something of an Internet cliché—the stuff of sneering "Worst Majors" listicles that seem always to be sponsored by personal-finance websites.

On the other hand, an impressive array of public figures are eager to give the exodus from the humanities an additional push. They know where public support for education has to be concentrated in order to yield tangible returns both for individuals and for the nation: the STEM disciplines (science, technology, engineering, and math). *These* are the degrees American business is screaming for. These are the fields of study that will give us "broadly shared economic prosperity, international competitiveness, a strong national defense, a clean energy future, and longer, healthier, lives for all Americans," as a White House press release put it in 2012.

Where does that leave the humanities, which don't contribute in any obvious way to national defense or economic prosperity? Writing in *Forbes* in May 2012, the management theorist and financier Peter Cohan proposed a course of straightforward erasure: "To fix this problem, the answer is simple enough: cut out the departments offering majors that make students unemployable." Certain red-state politicians seemed eager to take up the task. In 2013, Governor Pat McCrory, of North Carolina, dismissed disciplines like gender studies as elitist woolgathering and announced, "I'm going to adjust my education curriculum to what business and commerce needs." Governor Rick Scott of Florida declared that "we don't need a lot more anthropologists in the state," while a panel he convened in 2012 called for tuition prices to be subsidized for those willing to acquiesce to the needs of business and study practical things. Those who wanted to study stuff like divinity or Latin would have to pay ever more to indulge in their profligate pastimes.

And so the old battle is joined again: the liberal arts versus more remunerative studies. This time around, of course, the war is flavored by all the cynical stratagems of contemporary politics. Take the baseline matter of STEM degree holders, the ones who are supposedly in such high demand. According to a 2013 study by the Economic Policy Institute, there is actually no shortage of STEM workers in the United States—and by extension, no need for all the incentives currently on the table to push even more students into those fields. Oh, the business community's loud demand for a greater supply of STEM grads is real enough. But its motive is the same as it is when business lobbies for more H-1B visas: to keep wages down by means of an ever growing reserve of interchangeable workers. Only in this case the demands are being presented as a favor to students, who must be rescued from a lifetime of philology-induced uselessness.

A similar logic explains the larger attack on the humanities. In the past, perhaps, conservatives stumped for some idealized core curriculum or maybe even for the Great Books of Western Civ; but now that the option of demolishing these disciplines is on the table, today's amped-up right finds it rather likes the idea. After all, universities are not only dens of liberal iniquity but also major donors to the Democratic Party.* Chucking a few sticks of dynamite into their comfy world is a no-brainer for any politician determined to "defund the left."

Fans of the banality of evil might appreciate the language

---

* According to statistics compiled by Neil Gross in *Why Are Professors Liberal and Why Do Conservatives Care?*, the most left-leaning division of the American university is the social sciences, closely followed by the humanities.

with which this colossal act of vandalism is being urged upon us. The 2012 report of the blue-ribbon commission established by Rick Scott (it was actually called "Florida Blue-Ribbon Task Force") set about burying the humanities with a sandstorm of convoluted management talk.

> Four key policy questions must be addressed to accelerate Florida's progression toward world-class recognition as a system, particularly as its measurement framework transitions from simply reporting to collaborating toward clear goals. . . . Boards can advance effective cost management by helping to shape the conversation about aligning resources with goals and creating a culture of heightened sensitivity to resource management across the campus.

Let us assess the battle so far. In one corner, we have rhetoric like this: empty, pseudoscientific jargon rubberstamped by a chamber of commerce hack . . . who was appointed by the governor of Florida . . . who was himself elected thanks to the Tea Party. It is not merely weak, it is preposterous; it is fatuity at a gallop.

In the other corner, stepping up to defend itself, we have the university-level humanities. Stung by the attacks on their livelihood, the nation's leading humanists have closed ranks, taken up their pencils, and tried to explain why they exist. Unfortunately, the result is a train wreck of desperate rationalizations, clichés, and circular reasoning.

They insist that their work must not be judged by bogus metrics like the employability of recent graduates. They scold journalists for getting the story wrong in certain of its details. They express contempt for the dunces in state legislatures. They tear into the elected philistines who badger them with what the Harvard professor Homi Bhabha calls a "primitive and reductive view of what is essential."

And with touching earnestness, they argue that the humanities are *plenty* remunerative. They tell of CEOs who demand well-rounded young employees rather than single-minded, vocationally focused drudges. They remind us that humanities grads get into law and medical schools, which in turn lead (as everyone knows, right?) to the big money. Besides, they point out, the humanist promise of understanding our mysterious country draws foreign students—and foreign currency—to college towns across the land. They even play the trump card of national security: wouldn't we have done better in the global "war on terror" if we had trained more Arabic linguists prior to the start of hostilities?

Their mission, after all, is not about money: it is about molding young citizens for democracy! In making this traditional argument, no one today will venture quite as far as Bruce Cole, a former chairman of the National Endowment for the Humanities, who in 2004 claimed that the humanities were "part of our homeland defense." But we're pretty close.

Consider the 2013 report of the American Academy of Arts & Sciences, which asserts that our political system itself "depends on citizens who can think critically, understand their own history, and give voice to their beliefs while respecting the views of others." As proof, the authors of the report cite Thomas Jefferson's fondness for liberal education, and then proceed to trumpet the

humanities as nothing less than "the keeper of the republic"—
a phrase that is doubtless meant to out-patriot the various conservatives nipping at the academy's ankles.*

Others want nothing to do with such hackneyed arguments. Harvard University's effort to justify the high station
of the humanities, a dense and confusing text that was also issued
in 2013, insists that these disciplines are designed in part to
"unmask the operations of power," not to buttress them. The
document then disavows Harvard's *previous* justification for the
humanities, which had stressed the "civic responsibilities of
American citizens living in and aspiring to preserve a free democratic society." No, that was last century's model—jingoistic
junk. These days, the humanities are all about embracing ambiguity. As the Harvard humanists write:

> At the same time, therefore, that we aspire to ground our sense
> of ourselves on some stable understanding of the aim of life
> (e.g., the responsible citizen in a free society), we must con-
> stantly aspire to discover anew what the best way to charac-
> terize and cultivate such an aim might be. The humanities
> are the site where this tension is cultivated, nurtured, and
> sustained.†

---

* The very same month that the academy issued this report, its president was
found not to have earned the Ph.D. ascribed to her on the organization's
website.
† It gets more circular a few pages later when the authors declare: "An understanding of the power of the humanistic enterprise, therefore, and an understanding
of how responsibly to engage it and employ it, should be the central aims of any
education in the humanities."

The nurturing and sustaining of tensions—that's the stuff. Of course, some tensions are more desirable than others, and for all their excitement about the unmasking of power, the Harvard humanists have little interest in unmasking their own. Nor should their genuflection at the altar of ambiguity be taken as a call to knock down the disciplinary walls. No, according to an addendum to the Harvard report signed by Bhabha, even students interested in interdisciplinary studies will be D.O.A. unless they first encounter "disciplinary specificity *in its most robust expression.*" Ambiguity is a stern taskmaster, I guess.

Most touching, perhaps, is the argument advanced by the famous literary theorist Stanley Fish in a 2010 *New York Times* "Opinionator" column. After shooting down the many absurd defenses of the humanities that are floating around these days, Fish advises inhabitants of academia's more rarefied regions to forget even *trying* to explain themselves to the public. Don't ask what "French theory" does for the man in the street, Fish writes. Instead, ask whether its

> insights and style of analysis can be applied to the history of science, to the puzzles of theoretical physics, to psychology's analysis of the human subject. In short, justify yourselves to your colleagues, not to the hundreds of millions of Americans who know nothing of what you do and couldn't care less and shouldn't be expected to care.

Once, academics like Fish dreamed of bringing young people to a full understanding of their humanity, and maybe even of changing the world. Now their chant is: We're experts because other experts say we're experts. We critique because we critique because we critique—but all critique stops at the door to the faculty lounge.

One thing the defenders of the humanities don't talk about very much is the cost of it all. In the first chapter of her 2010 book *Not for Profit,* for example, the philosopher Martha Nussbaum declares that while the question of "access" to higher ed is an important one, "it is not, however, the topic of this book."

Maybe it should have been. To discuss the many benefits of studying the humanities absent the economic context in which the humanities are studied is to miss a pretty big point. When Americans express doubts about whether (in the words of the Obama pollster Joel Benenson) "a college education was worth it," they aren't making a judgment about the study of history or literature that needs to be refuted. They are remarking on its price.

Tellingly, not a single one of the defenses of the humanities that I read claimed that such a course of study was a good deal for the money. The Harvard report, amid its comforting riffs about ambiguity, suggests that bemoaning the price is a "philistine objection" not really worth addressing. The document produced by the American Academy of Arts & Sciences contains numerous action points for sympathetic legislators, but devotes just two paragraphs to the subject of student debt and tuition inflation, declaring blandly that "colleges must do their part to control costs," and then suggesting that the *real* way to deal with the problem is to do a better job selling the humanities.

Ignoring basic economics doesn't make them go away, however. The central economic fact of American higher ed today is this: it costs a lot. It costs a huge amount. It costs so much, in fact, that young people routinely start their postcollegiate lives with enormous debt loads.

This is the woolly mammoth in the room. I know that the story of how it got there is a complicated one. But regardless of how it happened, that staggering price tag has changed the way we make educational decisions. Quite naturally, parents and students alike have come to expect some kind of direct, career-prep transaction. They're out almost three hundred grand, for Christ's sake—you can't tell them it was all about embracing ambiguity. For that kind of investment, the gates to prosperity had better swing wide!

No quantity of philistine-damning potshots or remarks from liberal-minded CEOs will banish this problem. Humanists couldn't stop the onslaught even if they went positively retro and claimed their disciplines were needed to understand the mind of God and save people's souls. The turn to STEM is motivated by something else, something even more desperate and more essential than that.

What is required is not better salesmanship or more reassuring platitudes. The world doesn't need another self-hypnotizing report on why universities exist. What it needs is for universities to stop ruining the lives of their students. Don't propagandize for your institutions, professors. Change them. Grab the levers of power and pull.

(2013)

PART 3

THE POVERTY OF CENTRISM

Beltway Trifecta

There have been an estimated sixteen thousand books written about Abraham Lincoln. Like the lives of the wealthy and the secrets of self-improvement, a fascination with the Great Emancipator seems to be an unchanging feature of American literary taste. Few of these volumes, however, have had the resilience of Doris Kearns Goodwin's *Team of Rivals: The Political Genius of Abraham Lincoln*. In 2005, when the book first appeared, it was the subject of "vast critical acclaim" and remained on the *New York Times* bestseller list for some twenty-seven weeks, according to the press release that accompanied my copy. Three years later, a junior senator from Illinois named Barack Obama anointed *Team of Rivals* one of his favorite books, once again pushing it into the glare of public adulation. When Steven Spielberg transformed it into his movie *Lincoln* in 2012, the book climbed the charts for a third time.

Despite having triggered these sequential booms in Lincoln-iana, *Team of Rivals* is profoundly uninspiring. Goodwin's account doesn't provoke or startle with insight. Most of what she tells us has been told to us before—many, many times before. Indeed, the theme song from Ken Burns's *The Civil War* played invol-untarily in my head as I read, again, about the election of 1860, the Peninsula Campaign, the maneuvering in Washington over emancipation.

Goodwin's hypothesis is that the successes of the Lincoln administration were not a one-man accomplishment. No, the president had help, and he knew how to motivate people. It was Lincoln plus Secretary of State William Seward; Lincoln plus Attorney General Edward Bates; Lincoln plus Secretary of the Treasury Salmon P. Chase (you know, the man on the $10,000 bill). Which is to say, the Civil War was a *team effort,* in which men who didn't really like each other—political *rivals,* even—held important government jobs at the same time.

One cavil you might raise is that this isn't much of a revela-tion, since big wars are generally fought by national-unity gov-ernments. Nor was the "team of rivals" concept an innovation of the early 1860s, though Goodwin assures us it was. As the historian James Oakes pointed out in 2008, administrations incorporating the president's adversaries were commonplace in the early nineteenth century. They have been fairly common in our own time as well. During the Great Depression, for exam-ple, Franklin Roosevelt hired prominent men from the opposi-tion to fill cabinet posts, and almost every subsequent president has followed suit.

It was, in other words, an unremarkable arrangement, docu-mented here in a largely unremarkable book, all of it together about as startling as a Hallmark card. How did such a common-place slice of history come to define the political imagination of our time?

To begin with, the book perfectly captures the faiths of our white-collar priesthood. The appeal of *Team of Rivals* to this corporate demographic is built into its very architecture: after Goodwin relates some familiar Civil War anecdote, she invari-ably ties it to Lincoln's style of personnel management—this sup-posedly being the true manifestation of his genius. And to every vexing human-relations question, *Team of Rivals* gives a pat answer. How, for example, does one ride herd on a group of dif-ficult, contentious, even creative people? Goodwin's Lincoln offers the following counsel: Listen more and blame less. Also: Be sure to relax now and then. Also: Don't hold grudges.

"Lincoln's Leadership Lessons" was the headline that *Forbes* chose for a 2006 interview with Goodwin. When *Harvard Busi-ness Review* spoke to her in 2009, it called the article "Leader-ship Lessons from Abraham Lincoln"; *Fast Company's* take on the book was headlined "The Leadership Genius of Abraham Lincoln." When Goodwin herself addressed the annual conven-tion of the Society for Human Resource Management in 2008, she called her talk "HR Success Through [the] Lens of Lincoln."

I'm sorry I missed that presentation; it must have been enlightening. I suspect this because *Inc.* magazine has listed *Team of Rivals* as one of the "Best Leadership Books of All Time." Don-ald Trump, in his 2009 opus *Think Like a Champion*, includes it in his own recommended-reading list, as does the superconsul-tant Jim Collins. In truth, however, this last piece of critical acclaim shouldn't surprise anybody: as a blogger for the Man-powerGroup ("a world leader in workforce solutions") pointed out, "Lincoln personified the Level Five Leader immortalized in Jim Collins' *Good to Great*."

That was the initial phase of the book's rocketlike ascent into the middlebrow empyrean. The second stage, as I mentioned, came during the 2008 election season, after *Team of Rivals* was endorsed by Barack Obama. That's when it occurred to pundit after pundit that the book was about something that should properly warm the heart of every American: bipartisanship. The Obama/Lincoln comparison was suddenly the great cliché of the moment—it made the cover of *Time* in October of that year, and the cover of *Newsweek* in November. And once the election was over, the possibility of an executive-branch team of rivals became a fixation of our intellectual punditburo.

Soon they were busily quizzing one another as to whether each new cabinet nominee fit the "team of rivals" template. Hillary Clinton obviously did, and the same might be said of Larry Summers and the Republican Robert Gates. When Obama nominated another Republican, Judd Gregg, for commerce secretary, the Lincoln comparisons flew; when he sought out the opinions of his recent antagonist John McCain, they soared. In a conversation with Tom Brokaw, the NBC reporter Andrea Mitchell noted how *Team of Rivals* (by "our colleague and friend Doris Kearns Goodwin") had influenced Obama, then suggested some additional rivals the president-elect might care to embrace.

> He has John McCain coming tomorrow to Chicago. That is a very important step, they say. . . . There are others who have been mentioned: Chuck Hagel and, we know, Bob Gates at Defense, and other Republicans—his good friend Dick Lugar, who has not been persuaded to come to the State Department

so far. So he really sees this in a very bipartisan way, in the true spirit of that.

Mitchell's juxtaposition of "friends," "rivals," and "bipartisan" helps us understand the high-octane appeal of this plodding idea. To a Washington notable of the pre-Trump era, a team of rivals was a glorious thing: it meant that elections had virtually no consequences for members of the consensus. No one was sentenced to political exile because he or she was on the wrong side; the presidency changed hands, but all the players still got a seat at the table.

The only ones left out of this warm bipartisan circle of friendship were the voters, who woke up one fine day to discover that what they thought they'd rejected wasn't rejected in the least. And all in the name of Abraham Lincoln. Thanks for that, Abe.

Finally, stage three: Steven Spielberg signed on to what Goodwin was selling. His movie *Lincoln* focuses very narrowly on a short segment of the book in which the president rams the Thirteenth Amendment—the one abolishing slavery—through the House of Representatives. It's 1865, and Lincoln has just won reelection. Still, he doesn't want to wait for a new Congress to be seated: the amendment must be passed immediately. This means winning a two-thirds majority in a lame-duck legislative body that is still filled with his opponents, and the bulk of the movie is a close study of the lobbying and persuading and self-censoring to which Lincoln and his team must descend in order to, well, free the slaves. These are the lessons for our time that Spielberg has plucked from Goodwin's Lincoln saga.

And upon beholding the film, the upholders of the Washington consensus saw the clouds part and the sun shine through. Yet
another commonplace had been magnificently reaffirmed—and
this time it was the emptiest D.C. cliché of all. "It's compromise,"
is how Goodwin summarized the film's message for an inter-
viewer. And the commentariat chimed in unison: *Yes! We have
learned from this movie,* they sang, *that politicians must Make Deals.
That one must Give Something to Get Something.*

The film was a study in the "nobility of politics," declared
David Brooks in the *New York Times*; it teaches that elected
officials can do great things, but only if they "are willing to
bamboozle, trim, compromise and be slippery and hypocritical."
Michael Gerson of the *Washington Post* suggested that members
of Congress be made to watch the thing in order to acquire "a
greater appreciation for flexibility and compromise."* According
to Al Hunt of Bloomberg News, the film shows our greatest
president "doing what politicians are supposed to do, and today
too often avoid: compromising, calculating, horse trading, dealing and preventing the perfect from becoming the enemy of
a good objective." And here is an exchange about the movie
between David Gregory and—again!—Andrea Mitchell, two
Beltway Brahmins experiencing a miraculous mind meld on an
episode of *Meet the Press.*

---

* And lo! A screening was scheduled for the Senate on December 19, 2012.
The invitation from Harry Reid and Mitch McConnell, who had been at each
other's throats for many years, noted that the film "depicts the good which is
attainable when public servants put the betterment of the country ahead of
short-term political interests."

MITCHELL: Compromise is not a bad thing. And you—you
   feel that . . .

GREGORY: At a time when we so loathe politics . . .

MITCHELL: Exactly.

GREGORY: . . . so many people in this country.

MITCHELL: And it's become caricatured and demonized.

Those cruel caricatures—they're so unfair to compromise!
Thank goodness someone has rescued it from our sneering, cynical idealism.

The Civil War is a peculiar place to set such a message. After
all, it was compromise that permitted the South's slave empire to
grow so large—the Compromise of 1850, the Kansas-Nebraska
Act, and so on—and Abraham Lincoln first rose to prominence
as a highly moralistic opponent of the last of these. The abolition-
ist movement itself was about ninety-nine parts idealistic grassroots outrage to one part Washington machination. And the war
itself brought about a popular demand for "unconditional surrender," not further compromise with the South.

The movie actually goes well beyond celebrating compromise:
it also justifies corruption. Lincoln and his men, as they are
depicted here, do not merely buttonhole and persuade and cajole.
They buy votes outright with promises of patronage jobs and (it
is strongly suggested) cash bribes. The noblest law imaginable
is put over by the most degraded means. As Thaddeus Stevens,
leader of the Radical Republicans in the House of Representatives,
says after the amendment is finally approved: "The greatest measure of the nineteenth century was passed by corruption, aided
and abetted by the purest man in America."

The movie is fairly hard on crusading reformers like Thaddeus Stevens. The great lesson we are meant to take from his career is that idealists must learn to lie and to keep their mouths shut at critical moments if they wish to be effective. Lobbyists, on the other hand, are a class of people the movie takes pains to rehabilitate. Spielberg gives us a raffish trio of such men, hired for the occasion by William Seward, and they get the legislative job done by throwing money around, buying off loose votes—the usual. They huddle with Lincoln himself to talk strategy, and in a climactic scene, Spielberg shows us how a worldly lobbyist can *git-r-done* while a public servant dithers about legalisms. Happy banjo-and-fiddle music starts up whenever the lobbyists are on-screen—drinking, playing cards, dangling lucrative job offers—because, after all, who doesn't love a boodle-bundling gang of scamps?

Tony Kushner, the celebrated playwright who wrote the script for *Lincoln,* told NPR that the project had allowed him "to look at the Obama years through a Lincoln lens." As in 1865, he said, there is enormous potential now for "rebuilding a real progressive democracy in this country." There are "obstacles" to this project, however. And among the most notable ones, in Kushner's view, are those damn liberals—or, more specifically, "an impatience on the part of very good, very progressive people with the kind of compromising that you were just mentioning, the kind of horse trading that is necessary."

Allow me to do some historicizing of my own. Since about the middle of the Bush years, we have been living through a broad revival of reform sentiments. What ignited this revival, and what has kept it going since then, is a disgust with precisely the sort of workaday Washington horse trading that the makers of this movie have chosen to celebrate. Think of all the chapters in this saga of outrage: the soft-money campaign donations; the selling of earmarks; the Koch brothers and their galaxy of Washington pressure groups; the *Citizens United* decision; the power of money over the state.

I myself think it's healthy that public fury over this stuff has simmered on into the present; there's still plenty to be furious about. The lobbyists may be Democrats or Republicans, but they are pulling the wires for the same interests as always. Many of the people who engineered the deregulation of Wall Street (or their protégés) are still hanging around the halls of power. And the one great triumph of the Obama administration, health care reform, was flawed from the beginning, thanks to a heavy thumb on the scales placed by the insurance and pharmaceutical industries.

Maybe complaining about all this is yet another hangup of the contemporary Thaddeus Stevens set, who can't see that tremendous victories await if they'd just lighten up about reform and money-in-politics. But maybe—just maybe—reform *is itself* the great progressive cause. Maybe fixing the system must come first, as a certain senator from Illinois once seemed to believe, and everything else will follow from that.

Instead we have a movie that glorifies Abraham Lincoln as a great compromiser, focusing on the one episode where a dash of corruption worked wonders and everyone lucked out and the best measure in American history was thereby enacted. While watching it, though, I couldn't help but think of all the episodes of ordinary Washington venality that this movie effectively rationalizes—like the doings of the Grant administration, for example, in which several of the same characters who figure in

Lincoln played a role in one of the most corrupt eras in American history. Or just imagine a movie about the lobbyists who pushed banking deregulation through in the centrism-worshipping Clinton years. All the magic elements were there: consensus; compromise; idealists in surrender; lovable lobbyists dangling pleasures of the flesh before bureaucrats. Ninety minutes glorifying the merry japes of *those* lovable corruptionists—that's a task for a real auteur.

(2013)

The Animatronic Presidency

It is a good thing that politicians concern themselves with their legacy and the scrutiny of generations to come. In fact, I wish they worried about it more; I wish they constantly asked themselves and their advisers what the nation's future scholars will make of their decisions. It would be a robust check on an otherwise too-powerful office, where the decision to drop a bomb or render a suspect is attended by few other consequences.

Unfortunately, courting historical analysis is not the same thing as building presidential libraries, the museums that are the main object of our leaders' "legacy" projects. They aren't even in the same category, really. When I visited three of the most recent of these library/museums a while back—the William J. Clinton Presidential Center plus two museums commemorating the administrations of men named George Bush—I found them to be, by and large, institutions of bald propaganda, buildings on which hundreds of millions of dollars have been spent to cast, literally in stone, a given individual's personal war with reality.

All of the presidential museums I reference had certain basic things in common. Each contains a replica of the Oval Office as it was decorated when the museum's subject worked there. Each displays lots of formal White House dinner settings and gifts the president received from foreign leaders. Two of the three feature a presidential limousine or some other mode of official conveyance. And their object is always the same: to make you, the visitor, love and esteem the politician in question.

This is closer to advertising than it is to scholarship. And of course it can be persuasive. All three museums I visited were successful, to a certain degree, at convincing me to admire their subjects. I walked into each as the most skeptical possible visitor, ready to find fault and argue with the text. I didn't particularly like any of the three presidents in question, although I voted for Bill Clinton and I once gave a lecture at the University of Arkansas's nearby Clinton School of Public Service. But I left all three of these presidential shrines thinking the same thing of the man in question: *Dang, he sure seems like a good guy. Despite all his screwups, he must have meant well.*

Sometimes this warm feeling would stick to me all the way back to my hotel room, where I would finally wash it away with a cold six-pack.

Another thing these presidential libraries have in common is that they soft-pedal those moments of partisan rancor known as elections. Yes, each of them has lots of campaign buttons and the stupid sloganeering memorabilia you can collect at party conventions, but usually this stuff is sequestered in a single room or display case with little more explanation than a few common-places quoted from a campaign book. The implication is that no president is proud of what he did to get people to vote for him. The less said about elections, the better. Now, on to the *important* stuff, which is to say the big decisions and uplifting remarks that our subject made while he sat in the Oval Office.

In the George H. W. Bush Presidential Library and Museum in College Station, Texas, you will find nothing in the collections on display about "voodoo economics," the cruelly apt label that Bush applied to Ronald Reagan's doctrines while on the campaign trail in 1980. You will search his museum in vain for a reference to either his infamous Willie Horton TV commercial or the flag-veneration fury stoked by Bush and his adviser Lee Atwater, even though both episodes from the 1988 election are regarded by historians as milestones on the road to the culture-war bottom. Instead, the main commentary on that year's contest is delivered by George's wife, Barbara, who appears in a video testifying to her husband's many personal virtues. When this fine fellow George Bush finally lost in 1992, the museum makes clear, it was only because of public misapprehension of economic issues.

Visit the Bill Clinton museum in Little Rock, Arkansas, however, and you will find that the public of 1992 got matters exactly right, that they perceptively grasped that "it was Bill Clinton who claimed the mantle as the candidate of change," whatever that means. To judge by the library's orientation movie, the most urgent issue facing the nation in 1992 was, as Clinton himself puts it, "We've got to be one country again."

The exception to this Law of Meaningless Elections should

be the presidency of George W. Bush; after all, he won the presidency in 2000 only after a contest so close it brought on a constitutional crisis. And sure enough, at the George W. Bush Presidential Library and Museum in Dallas there is a large exhibit on that very subject, complete with examples of the Florida ballots that proved so controversial and an endless video loop of media errors on election night. But once again, what is not emphasized is what is most important, in this case the awkward but essential fact that George W. Bush actually received fewer votes than his opponent. I could find no mention in the museum at all of Bush *fils*'s ugly, Swiftboating triumph of 2004.

I was going to criticize this aspect of presidential libraries for the obvious reason that elections aren't some afterthought to be dismissed with empty phrases; they are, or should be, the very essence of politics.

On second thought, maybe there is something wholesome about the way these museums downplay partisan conflict. I personally find it irksome to sit in a chair and relive the elder George Bush's inaugural address, easily one of the most fatuous orations of the twentieth century. (Remember? "A thousand points of light.") But other people—like, say, the consensus-minded folks who write newspaper columns—no doubt find it reassuring and even inspiring to hear that disagreements aren't real. The way George H. W. Bush's museum presents him, this sneering culture warrior comes off like a fair and decent individual, especially when you compare the exhibits in his shrine to, say, the contumely that issues these days from the mouth of his fellow Texan Ted Cruz. Maybe presidential libraries are the last bastion of American civility, and I should just acknowledge that and stop typing right now.

It is the presidential library of Bush's son Dubya that makes such an approach impossible, because—just like the man himself in real life—his museum uses a surface of friendly platitudes and pseudo-professional objectivity to smuggle in distortion and self-interest of the crudest sort. This is apparent from one of the first exhibits the visitor comes to, "Creating Opportunity," which is supposedly about Bush's stewardship of the economy. Look closer, however, and it's actually a salute to a single economic tool—tax cuts—and it's so oblivious to the economic disaster that befell the country during the Bush years that it includes a hands-on display for kids teaching them "How tax relief helps small businesses grow the economy." There is, of course, no display on how Bush policies helped the really big businesses on Wall Street shrink the economy, even though that would be closer to historical reality.

I don't envy the people who won the contract to design Dubya's museum. His reign saw so many catastrophes to gloss over, so many screwups to minimize, and so many blunders to skate past that it must have taxed the imagination of the cleverest PR professionals. The basic problem facing them, of course, was how to present this stuff without making Bush seem like a scoundrel and without bringing visitors to an explosive rage. The strategy they appear to have settled upon is to defuse each discrete Bush disaster by presenting it between slabs of noncontroversial Bush virtue, sort of like the cadmium control rods that separate the radioactive material in a nuclear reactor.

And so the infuriating exhibit on tax cuts is followed by a heroic, day-by-day reconstruction of Bush's activities during his single chapter of greatness after September 11, 2001. Then: "Defending Freedom," which is to say, invading Afghanistan and Iraq, passing the Patriot Act, opening the prison at Guantánamo Bay, and all the obscene rest of it. If you read carefully, you will find the Iraq War concession you're looking for: "No stockpiles of WMD were found." Otherwise, the museum sticks closely to the old script. The Iraq invasion was part of a "Global War on Terror"; we did it "to enforce the will of the international community"; and Saddam Hussein was really, really bad. Besides, remember that time when the grateful Iraqis tore down that statue? How they dipped their fingers in purple ink when they voted?

This thick stuff is chased by lighter memories of Laura and the twins and all the fun they had. Barney the dog capers once again on the White House lawn. There's an exhibit on the President's Malaria Initiative, which I had never heard of before but which has obvious merit as a disgust suppressant. And there's a sycophantic letter from Bono, written on *Vanity Fair* letterhead and carefully preserved for all eternity in a glass case.

Then, it's back to the awful. An exhibit on Hurricane Katrina—or, more precisely, on how the lousy response to the hurricane wasn't really Bush's fault. An exhibit on the financial crisis, which, the president tells us, was "not a failure of the free market system." Then comes the museum's most ingenious device for blame evasion: "Decision Points Theater," an exhibit in which the greatest blunders of the past decade are presented as a sort of video game. In the scenario on the screen when I was there, visitors watched frantic TV news footage from the worst days of the 2008 financial crisis and were presented with two choices: bail the bankers out or let the bastards fail—

because those were the only two possibilities, right? If you think Bush screwed things up, well, let's see you get a higher score than he did.

By the way, the group I watched chose to let the Wall Street banks fail, a satisfying denouement that is popular with the visitors, a nearby guard told me.

What I am saying is that this is a museum whose entire pedagogical objective is to get one man off the hook for his egregious misrule. Maybe all presidential libraries do this; maybe it's only more noticeable here since Iraq is still in flames and Wall Street banks are still fleecing the world and Bush's executive-branch wrecking crew has resumed its experiment in good government. But before your revulsion can boil over, you find yourself learning about the remarkable virtues of the George W. Bush retirement. His library, mirabile dictu, has a Platinum LEED rating. He himself helped to build a humble clinic in Africa in 2012 and has arranged many sporting events for wounded veterans.* Maybe you'll even buy the jigsaw puzzle they're selling in the gift shop that shows Bush and seven other Republican presidents playing cards, all of them lost in hilarious bonhomie. Forgive this man, please!

After all the blame evasion, all the gaping lacunae and strutting Texicity of the two Bush presidential libraries, it is something of a relief to visit the Bill Clinton Presidential Center. The

---

* He also painted portraits of wounded vets and published them in a 2017 book that was clearly meant to rehabilitate his reputation.

superficial contrasts are big. Architecturally, the Bush museums are low-slung, limestone-heavy affairs, while the Clinton shrine is an elevated glass-and-steel box propped up on stilts at one end. Furthermore, Bill Clinton is not anxious to prove that he's a bona fide, red-blooded Arkansan, as the Bushes are with their home state. Clinton can take that status safely for granted.

Another noteworthy difference: Clinton seems almost proud of what he did as president. The museum comes at you with a hailstorm of details, far more information than any visitor can possibly absorb; among other things, it includes a collection of notebooks showing Clinton's exact whereabouts on every single day of his presidency. The detail gets even more granular on the days surrounding his 1993 inauguration, which the visitor is invited to relive hour by hour. There is also an electronic stock-ticker sign recalling the market's enthusiasm for Clinton's governance, and a chart showing employment during the years of his administration in which the upward-sloping line is represented by a proudly glowing pink neon tube.

But this impulse to document can be just as deceptive in its own way as the conspicuous silences favored by the Bush family. What is presented so voluminously at the Clinton Center is really just a highly detailed collection of talking points—a stroll down a New Democrat memory lane that is lined with slogans at every turn.

For me, what it all brought back was how contemptuous the White House could be toward traditional liberals as Team Clinton made consensus out of one Republican idea after another. Consider, for example, the library's exhibit on NAFTA, entitled "Expanding Our Shared Prosperity." The really subtle idea that is presented here is that "trade" is a good thing. Not that some particular *kind* of trade or *level* of trade or *set of rules* for trade is a good thing, but just that "trade" is good, full stop, and that therefore the two-thousand-page document that is NAFTA must also be good. (As the former U.S. trade representative Charlene Barshefsky puts it in a video recording, "I don't know of any country that has grown without trade.") The tacit disdain for the viewer's intelligence is remarkable, even as the museum flatters us with those great heaps of pointless data.

Then again, this combination of flattery and contempt for the little people is also how Clinton ruled the country. The experts and the bankers had the answers to our problems, Clinton knew, and therefore his job was to sell those answers, to marshal the unruly rank and file of the Democratic Party behind the solutions that every educated person agreed to be correct. He promised to give us "an administration that looks like America," but his brave multicultural bunch then proceeded to deregulate Wall Street. He would tell us he was promoting "learning across America," and then do all he could to open charter schools. He would say he was "making work pay" and then bequeath us a nation where workers have no power and only ownership pays.

What is worthwhile and in earnest at this museum is the narration that visitors listen to on a handheld device, in which Bill Clinton himself tells the story of his life. As you listen, all the deception and the centrist cant seems to fall away, and you are hearing a fascinating man relate genuinely profound insights that date all the way back to when he was three years old. It was only after listening to this that I began to think about the design of the Clinton Center itself—this oddly shaped box that is propped up at one end by a pair of poles that appear to be far too small for the job. The official explanation for this peculiar structure is that it is supposed to look like a bridge, and that's appropriate, see, because (in another famous bit of fatuous oratory) Bill Clinton once mentioned a bridge to the twenty-first century, and here we are in the twenty-first century, and so this building reminds us to give thanks to the guy who got us here.

But if you ask me, this thing doesn't look like a bridge at all. What it most obviously resembles, as the longtime Clinton critic Robert Borosage pointed out to me, is a shipping container, a glass-and-light version of one of those big steel boxes you see zooming through your town on trains and piled up by the thousands in former industrial hubs. Sending American manufacturing to other lands was Bill Clinton's greatest legacy—a venture that destroyed the power of unions and advanced the enlightened white-collar project of "globalization," as he and his team called it—and his museum is designed to remind us of this achievement. There it sits, up on its pedestal: a light-and-glass shipping container, levitating in the night sky over Little Rock, the enlightened instrument that took your livelihood away.

Next it will be Barack Obama's turn to contemplate his legacy. Indeed, according to newspaper stories on the subject, Obama's team began planning for his postpresidential career only a few months after he started his second term as president. According to the *New York Times,* the job of coordinating this work was regarded within the White House as a particularly desirable "plum," even as a "hot property."

What made it "hot" was that it was surrounded by money on all sides. Once upon a time, presidential libraries were fairly modest structures. Harry Truman's cost $1.7 million. George W. Bush, however, required some $500 million to build his propaganda theater. Of course, opening a presidential center is not exactly the same thing as running a political campaign, but when such enormous sums are involved it raises the same question of whether donors might have received something in exchange for their contribution. Perhaps presidential libraries, with their huge price tags, serve to keep presidents beholden to the wealthy right on into their lame-duck years.

In Obama's case, a team of businesspeople organized the legacy project from outside the White House. Various cities and institutions put together their bids for the future Obama library, each of them competing to offer the sweetest deal and the finest piece of real estate. And, of course, political donors had to be tapped one more time—so many of them that, according to the *New York Times*'s 2013 story on the subject, an investment banker who was close to the president said Obama was "show[ing] more 'good will' to the business community" because of the looming need to raise hundreds of millions of dollars from them.

The possibility of Obama catering to the wealthy on into his postpresidential future is one reason to find all this legacy planning objectionable. Another is the spectacle of cities and universities bidding for his future library in the way desperate heartland towns bid for conventions and footloose pro sports franchises.

But the main reason I wish Obama would lay off the monumentalizing is because we don't need another one. These fake museums are beneath him. They are closer to exercises in personal triumphalism than chronicles of an era. The presidents I have described here were not the equivalent of Napoleon, but every one of them has built the equivalent of a vainglorious Invalides for himself.

A hundred years from now, these museums themselves will be the objects of study. Students visiting them will learn not that, say, George W. Bush was without fault, but will marvel instead at the desperate blame evasion that is built into the very architecture of his presidential library, and they will discuss what this tells us about his disastrous approach to governing.

Anyone can make a museum. The byways of America are cluttered with homemade displays of folk art and hobbies taken to extremes. Sometimes they are profound, sometimes they are political, but always they are intensely personal.

What separates them from these hundred-million-dollar presidential piles? Not much, really. For all the fund-raising that goes into these monuments, all the landscaping, all the careful weighing of phrases, the result is far closer to the Hall of Presidents at Disney World than to the Smithsonian. In fact, I've read that the Lyndon Johnson library has an animatronic LBJ; I haven't seen it myself, but until a few years ago it was reportedly dressed like a cowboy and told colorful anecdotes while leaning on a fence. And maybe that's the right way to go about these things: let the folks from the Magic Kingdom handle the job.

(2014)

Bully Pulpit

It makes perfect sense that Andrew Breitbart's last month on this earth—or at least one representative moment of it—was documented in a much played YouTube video. The setting is the lawn outside Washington's Marriott Wardman Park, where the right-wing Internet impresario, who died at age forty-three in March 2012, had just given a speech to the adoring throng at the Conservative Political Action Conference. Now, upon leaving the hotel, Breitbart discovers that CPAC is besieged by protesters from Occupy D.C.

The video clip, shot by somebody in the crowd, initially shows protesters banging on a drum and chanting one of those "Hey hey, ho ho" routines. The camera then pans left and comes across a man with longish white hair and a beard, like Santa Claus with prominent canines and a permanent snarl. It is Breitbart, and he is yelling something: *"Behave* yourself! *Behave* your-self!" It is a line from one of the RoboCop movies, and Breitbart screams it again and again and again, clinging to the words even as a couple of real-life cops temporarily nudge him out of the frame.

Then something clever occurs to the protesters. They change tempo and take up a different chant, which seems specifically aimed at their screaming tormentor: "Racist, sexist, antigay! Right-wing bigot, go away!" Then something clever occurs to Breitbart. Picking up the pace, he begins shouting: "Stop *raping* people! Stop *raping* people!"

And that, I submit, is what American political discourse looked like in 2012—as conducted by the nation's most tech-savvy, Internet-enlightened factions. To note that these factions were speaking past each other is to utter a crushing under-statement. These were people so cocooned in self-righteousness that they had no interest in what their opposite numbers really thought. Their cherished caricatures of the other side— alternately racist or rapist—were all that mattered.

This bizarre showdown was not out of character for Andrew Breitbart. It wasn't an ugly incident that marred an otherwise respectable career. On the contrary, it was the very sort of thing his followers admired him for doing. Breitbart loved to confront protesters, to bellow at people in public places, to call journal-ists ugly names. He tweeted constantly, insultingly, fighting with his antagonists on Twitter right up to the hour of his death. He would while away the hours fantasizing about an armed civil war against liberals, insisting that such a conflict would be entirely justified, since (in his mind) conservatives were the great victims of American life and liberals were "the bullies on the play-ground."

But these things are not what make Andrew Breitbart worth writing about. There are dozens of right-wing loudmouths with high media profiles. There are thousands of jerks on Twitter. And there are millions of conservatives who see themselves as victims. Breitbart was something different: a man who started from gen-uinely critical premises and went haywire somewhere down the line.

I met him just once, while we were both waiting to appear on a TV program, and was surprised to discover that he was a fairly decent fellow when the cameras were turned off. I was fur-ther surprised to learn—although I can't recall the conversa-tional turn that brought us to the subject—that he shared my admiration for *Spy* magazine, which prosecuted an endless war against the nation's celebrities during the eighties and nineties by means of pranks and creative derision.

The connection seems obvious in retrospect. Breitbart's single greatest moment as a political troublemaker involved a *Spy*-style prank: a series of hidden-camera interviews from 2009 in which two young right-wing provocateurs got employees of the neighborhood-activist group ACORN to offer advice on get-ting started in the prostitution business. The videos didn't expose the delusions of the powerful, as classic pranks are sup-posed to do; they targeted a group that represented poor people. What the videos felt like was the work of daring college kids who had gone slumming and would now report back on all the crazy stuff they heard. Still, the stuff those kids heard was undeniably crazy, and the firestorm that followed, ginned up resourcefully by Breitbart, proved too toxic for ACORN to overcome.[*]

The aspect of *Spy* that I loved most was its contempt for celebrity, its gleeful smashing of our modern-day idols. And this is what Andrew Breitbart thought he was all about, at least in the beginning. It is not clear from his articles, books, or blustering speeches that the man really shared or even understood the broader concerns of the political movement that lionized him. But when the subject was Hollywood, Breitbart's hate ran pure. He was a native son of upper-middle-class Los Angeles, and trashing the lazy assumptions and comfy prejudices of his fellow Angelenos seems to have been his life project.

In 2004, Breitbart published *Hollywood, Interrupted: Insanity Chic in Babylon,* which he coauthored with Mark Ebner, *Spy*'s West Coast man and a journalist whose work I particularly relished when I was young. The book was a product, Ebner explained to me, of the two men's "mutual loathing for Hollywood and celebrity." Elsewhere, Breitbart described the pathological self-absorption of his hometown like this:

> The people who come to L.A. saw *Beverly Hills, 90210* or a variation on that theme, and so that's how they act there.

---

[*] The mainstream media were an indirect victim of the prank. The ACORN videos were heavily edited and included knee-slapping intros featuring one of the pranksters duded up in a pimp costume worthy of a seventies blaxploitation film. In truth, the prankster wore ordinary street clothes when visiting the ACORN offices.

Or they see *Entourage*. So you have bad actors coming to Hollywood bad-acting the part of what they think Hollywood is like. So you have really insecure people in a non-meritocracy where it's all about your relationships, who are vicious backstabbers, who don't think you should be dating somebody. It's like an orgy of people climbing over each other to stick it into the next orifice.

I know, Hollywood was vain and shallow long before *90210* first aired in the early nineties. But every now and then we need to be reminded what a vale of pretense and putrefaction the culture industry is. Had I been raised in its narcissistic demesne, I sometimes think, I might have become a confrontational right-winger myself.

Hating Hollywood was Andrew Breitbart's starting point, and as his career unfolded he simply built out from there, making Hollywood's venality into the central problem of the world. The film industry, he argued, was somehow prior to or determinative of everything else that goes on in America. *"Hollywood is more important than Washington,"* he announced in his 2011 memoir, *Righteous Indignation: Excuse Me While I Save the World!* "What happens in front of the cameras on a soundstage at the Warner Bros. lot often makes more difference to the fate of America than what happens in the back rooms of the Rayburn House Office Building on Capitol Hill."

This, then, was Breitbart's political theory. Start with the unquestionable fact that Hollywood is liberal, in a kind of foggy lifestyle way, and that this liberalism trickles down via the royalist workings of celebrity culture. Add to this the belief that Hollywood is all-powerful, and the obvious conclusion is that spoiled actors are responsible for what ails America. You can ignore the postindustrial havoc masterminded by Chicago School economists and the wars waged by hard-bitten Beltway neocons. What really matters is those damned movie stars and their shallow longing for ancient grains and peace in Darfur.

Perhaps it is inevitable that a son of Brentwood would believe Hollywood holds supreme power over American life. This is, after all, what Hollywood itself tells us: that to live a life beyond the camera's gaze is never to have lived at all.

It's also an idea that occurs naturally to anyone raised in the pale blue TV light of twentieth-century America—like me, for example. When I was younger, I would probably have agreed with Breitbart's oft-repeated claim that "politics is downstream from culture." I thought that advertising directed our consumer habits, that rock stars made our mores, and that newspaper people set our political agenda; that they were, all of them, unmoved movers accountable to no one.

But of course it doesn't work that way. I eventually discovered that there was something even more important than movies in determining what happens in Washington, and in every town in the United States: Business. Profits. Gain. In fact, to try to understand American life without recognizing the significance of business is to deny its essence, its motive force. It is to talk about cars without mentioning motors, or gasoline, or roads.

Understanding this is a step that Breitbart, like most of his friends on the right, was never able to take. He talked constantly, in his ultra-cynical way, of a "Democrat-Media Complex"—a sort of pumped-up liberal-bias Leviathan—but as far as I can tell, he never took his cynicism beyond that. It didn't dawn on him that Hollywood's vaunted liberalism might be just for show, an expression of some deeper (and yet shallower) industry need, no more meaningful than, say, its desire to see the little people of the world using hemp bags to cart their stuff home from Whole Foods.

This left Breitbart with a worldview that was both totally politicized—in which every stray anchorman comment was a work of fiendish propaganda—and yet completely superficial. He was a great collector of grievances, of the stupid things said by people on TV. But the actual substance of controversy mattered little. Every question was to be debated at the second remove (*What are the media saying about it?*) and every debate could be understood as a succession of mean names each side called the other, with a fail-safe winning argument: *The liberals started it!*

For example, when describing the lead-up to the Iraq War in *Righteous Indignation,* Breitbart unreels a long list of dumb things uttered in 2002 and 2003 by Hollywood liberals, then informs us that these silly people pushed their antiwar vision through the media "unchallenged." And that's pretty much it. That's his version of how we got into the Iraq War, with its trillion-dollar price tag and its tens of thousands of corpses and its ruination of that country. You, reader, might recall debates over WMDs and administration hints of Saddam's culpability for 9/11, but to judge by his memoir, Breitbart pretty much missed all that. For him, it was all about liberals calling conservatives names.

Or consider the 1991 Supreme Court confirmation hearings of Clarence Thomas, which Breitbart often cited as the origin of his conservatism: as the hypocritical liberals huffed and puffed and persecuted the nominee, the blinders fell from the young

Angeleno's eyes. However, when Breitbart told this story of his epiphany to the sixties troublemaker Paul Krassner (the people at *Playboy* put these two Katzenjammer Kids in a room together), Krassner responded with a sheaf of repugnant opinions Thomas had subsequently rendered from the bench. Now Breitbart dodged the question. He knew nothing about those. An offensive TV moment twenty years ago was what really mattered.

Putting aside his Hollywood-hating crusade, the central idea of Breitbart's career was to depict liberals as a tribe of false accusers always painting the world—to quote that Occupy D.C. chant—as "racist, sexist, antigay." Of these three, the charge of racism was the favorite, not to mention the most potent, and Breitbart's goal was to neutralize the strategy once and for all.

What brought him closest to achieving this ambition, ironically, was becoming a false accuser himself. In July 2010, one of Breitbart's websites posted video excerpts from an address to the NAACP by Shirley Sherrod, a Department of Agriculture official in Georgia. The speech, as it was edited, seemed to show Sherrod making a startling admission of racism toward a white farmer who came to her for help. In reality, Sherrod had gone on to tell how she overcame her prejudices, realized the common predicament of poor people regardless of race, and tried to save the white man's farm. But the complete video did not surface until the next day—and in the meantime, the right's infinite-repeat machine had been switched on, Sherrod had been fired by a panicking USDA, and the bias spotters had already advanced to the second remove, criticizing the mainstream media for not being sufficiently critical of the supposedly racist bureaucrat. Then it all fell apart. Apologies ensued, and Sherrod was offered another government job—which she declined, preferring to sue the neatly pressed khakis off Breitbart instead. (The suit was settled in 2015 for an unknown amount.)

So, too, did it go with Breitbart's larger war on celebrity. He started out as a man who loved to puncture Hollywood vanity, then became a VIP himself. "Media is everything," he used to say, and by the end it was all he was—a caricature, as he reportedly confided in his final days to the sixties radical Bill Ayers. His articles and books, like the Supreme Court decisions of Clarence Thomas, were secondary and are now largely forgotten. What will be remembered is the ranting collection of pixels he leaves behind, those images of a stout man with wild eyes and a snarling lip, saying something mean to someone.

As for Breitbart's relationship with his one true love, the Internet, I think it is best demonstrated by recalling the way he once quarreled with a *Gawker* editor via text message for three days. On and on the mighty champions fought, ultimately generating some ten thousand words between them while trying to hash out whether neo-Nazis could be described as right-wing. Here was an endless Iron Butterfly drum solo of pointless speculation and wandering rage, with no pauses to acknowledge things that are obvious to everyone or to check history books that might have cleared matters up quickly. Just two voices screaming at each other in the ether, their petty insults and accusations preserved for future generations.

For decades now, the Breitbart model of political confrontation has been around in one form or another. The more I look back over its history, the more I am convinced that its closest evolutionary relative is pro wrestling. There are the same mock feuds, the same posturing outrage, with the antagonists always avenging their vain selves or the wounded honor of their stage friends. The conflicts mean nothing. There is nothing at stake. And in the end there is nothing to remember.

Once upon a time I thought there might be something admirable about Andrew Breitbart's hatchet-wielding campaign against the happy tree house of Hollywood complacency. But he never really delivered on the promise of his early days. As his career unfolded, he chose to sluice his high-octane scorn not against the powerful but against the traditionally powerless. His skirmishes with ACORN, with unions, with Shirley Sherrod—these were not the acts of a brave cultural renegade. They were merely dirty Republican tricks, deserving of an epithet that Breitbart wholeheartedly embraced: Nixonesque.

(2012)

The Powers That Were

All politicians love to complain about the press. They complain for good reasons and for bad. They cry over frivolous slights and legitimate inquiries alike. They moan about bias. They talk to friendlies only. They manipulate reporters and squirm their way out of questions. And this all makes perfect sense, because politicians and the press are, or used to be, natural enemies.

Conservative politicians have built their hostility toward the press into a full-blown theory of liberal media bias, a pseudosociology that is today the obsessive pursuit of certain nonprofit foundations, the subject matter of an annual crop of books, and the beating heart of a successful cable news network. Donald Trump, the current leader of the right's war against the media, hates this traditional foe so much that he banned a number of news outlets from attending his campaign events in 2016 and denounced the prestige media as bearers of "fake news." He did this even though he owes his prominence almost entirely to his career as a TV celebrity and to the news media's morbid fascination with his glowering mug.

His Democratic opponent in 2016 hated the press, too. Hillary Clinton may not have a general theory of right-wing media bias to fall back on, but she knows that she has been the subject of lurid journalistic speculation for decades. Back in the nineties, she watched her husband's presidency come under siege in an endless series of scandals and fake scandals, many of them featuring her as a kind of diabolical villainess, and in 2016 she took pains to stay well clear of press conferences. After losing to Donald Trump, she blamed the news media in part for her loss. She did this even though the editorial boards of the country's largest newspapers endorsed her over Trump by an unprecedented ratio of fifty-seven to two.

But it was the news media's attitude toward yet a third politician, Senator Bernie Sanders of Vermont, that best revealed the peculiar politics of the media in this time of difficulty and transition (or, depending on your panic threshold, industry-wide apocalypse) for newspapers.

To refresh your memory, the Vermont senator is an independent who likes to call himself a democratic socialist. He ran for the nomination on a platform of New Deal–style economic interventions such as single-payer health insurance, a regulatory war on big banks, and free tuition at public universities. Sanders was well to the left of where modern Democratic presidential candidates ordinarily stand, and in most elections he would have been dismissed as a marginal figure, more petrified wood than presidential timber.

But 2016 was different. It was a volcanic year, with the

middle class erupting over a recovery that didn't include them and over the obvious indifference of Washington, D.C., toward the economic suffering in vast reaches of the country.

For once, a politician like Sanders seemed to have a chance with the public. He won a stunning victory over Hillary Clinton in the New Hampshire primary, and despite his advanced age and avuncular finger-wagging, he was wildly popular among young voters. Eventually he was flattened by the Clinton juggernaut, of course, but Sanders managed to stay competitive almost all the way to the California primary in June.

His chances with the prestige press were considerably more limited. Before we go into details here, let me confess: I was a Sanders voter, and even interviewed him back in 2014, so perhaps I am naturally inclined to find fault in others' reporting on his candidacy. Perhaps it was the very particular media diet I was on in the first half of 2016, which consisted of daily megadoses of the *New York Times* and the *Washington Post* and almost nothing else. Even so, I have never before seen the press take sides as it did that year, openly and even gleefully bad-mouthing candidates who did not meet with its approval.

This shocked me when I first noticed it. The news stories seemed to go out of their way to mock Sanders or to twist his words, while the op-ed pages, which of course don't pretend to be balanced, seemed to be of one voice in denouncing my candidate. A *New York Times* article greeted the Sanders campaign in December 2015 by announcing that the public had moved away from his signature issue of the crumbling middle class. "Americans are more anxious about terrorism than income inequality," the paper declared—nice try, liberal, and thanks for playing. In March, the *Times* was caught making a number of

postpublication tweaks to a news story about the senator, changing what had been a sunny tale of his legislative victories into a
darker account of his outrageous proposals. When Sanders was
finally defeated in June, the same paper waved him goodbye
with a bedtime-for-Grandpa headline: "Hillary Clinton Made
History, but Bernie Sanders Stubbornly Ignored It."

I decided to approach this question by examining the opinion pages of the *Washington Post,* the conscience of the nation's
political class and one of America's few remaining first-rate news
organizations. The *Post*'s investigative and beat reporting are some
of the best in the world. The paper's chronicling of the political
life of the capital is without equal.

The *Post*'s opinion pages are a different matter, though. Pundits do not aim to be nonpartisan. They do not show "media bias"
in the traditional sense. But maybe the traditional definition
needs to be updated. We live in an era of reflexive opinionating
and quasi opinionating, and we derive much of our information
about the world from websites that have blurred the distinc-
tion between reporting and commentary, or else obliterated
it completely. For many of us, this ungainly hybrid *is* the news.
What matters, in any case, is that all the pieces I review here,
whether they appeared in pixels or in print, bear the imprimatur
of the *Washington Post,* the publication that defines the limits of
the permissible in the capital city.

Why should anyone care today that certain pundits were unkind
to Bernie Sanders? The election is long over. His campaign is,
as we like to say, history. Still, I think that what befell the Vermont senator at the hands of the *Post* should be of interest to all

of us. For starters, it represents a challenge to the standard theory of liberal bias. Sanders was, obviously, well to the left of Hillary Clinton, and yet that did not protect him from the ferocious scorn of the *Post,* a paper that media-hating conservatives regard as a sort of liberal death squad. Nor was Sanders undone by some seedy journalistic obsession with scandal or pseudoscandal. On the contrary, his record seems to have been remarkably free of public falsehoods, security-compromising email screwups, suspiciously large paychecks for pedestrian speeches, tape-recorded boasts about groping women, or any of that stuff.

An alternative hypothesis is required for what happened to Bernie Sanders, and I want to propose one that takes into account who the media are in these rapidly changing times. As we shall see, for the sort of people who write and edit the opinion pages of the *Post,* there was something deeply threatening about Sanders and his political views. He seems to have represented something that could not be spoken of directly but that clearly needed to be suppressed.

Who are those people? Let us think of them in the following way. The *Washington Post,* with its constant calls for civility, with its seemingly genetic predisposition for bipartisanship and consensus, is more than the paper of record for the capital; it is the house organ of a meritocratic elite, which views the federal city as the arena of its professional practice. Many of its leading personalities hail from a fairly exalted socioeconomic background (as is the case at most important American dailies). Its pundits are not workaday chroniclers of high school football games or city council meetings. They are professionals in the full sense of the word, well educated and well connected, often flaunting insider credentials of one sort or another. They are, of course, a comfortable bunch. And when they look around at the comfortable, well-educated folks who work in government, academia, Wall Street, medicine, and Silicon Valley, they see their peers.[*]

Now, consider the recent history of the Democratic Party. Beginning in the 1970s, it has increasingly become an organ of this same class. Affluent white-collar professionals are today the voting bloc that Democrats represent most faithfully, and they are the people whom Democrats see as the rightful winners in our economic order. Hillary Clinton, with her fantastic résumé and her life of striving and her much-commented-on qualifications, represented the aspirations of this class almost perfectly. An accomplished lawyer, she was in with the foreign-policy in crowd; she had the respect of leading economists; she was a familiar face to sophisticated financiers. She knew how things worked in the capital. To members of the highly educated, white-collar cohort, she was not just a candidate but a colleague, the living embodiment of their professional worldview.

In Bernie Sanders and his "political revolution," on the other hand, these same professionals saw something kind of horrifying: a throwback to the low-rent Democratic politics of many decades ago. Sanders may refer to himself as a progressive, but to the affluent white-collar class, what he represented was atavism, a regression to a time when demagogues in rumpled

---

[*] The professionalization of journalism is a well-known historical narrative, told by Timothy Crouse in *The Boys on the Bus* (1973), by David Halberstam in *The Powers that Be* (1979), and by James Fallows in *Breaking the News* (1996). The latter book, in particular, describes how journalism went from being "a high working-class activity" to an occupation for "college boys" in the mid-1960s.

jackets pandered to vulgar public prejudices against banks and capitalists and foreign factory owners.

Choosing Clinton over Sanders was a no-brainer for this group. It was not a matter of liberalism but of basic class identification. The people I am describing like to think they understand modern economics, and that they know better than to fear Wall Street or free trade. And they addressed themselves to the Sanders campaign by doing what professionals always do: defining the boundaries of legitimacy, by which I mean, defining Sanders out.

After reading through some two hundred *Post* editorials and op-eds about Sanders published between January and June 2016, I found a very basic disparity. Of the *Post* stories that could be said to take an obvious stand, the negative outnumbered the positive roughly five to one.* (Opinion pieces about Hillary Clinton, by comparison, came much closer to a fifty-fifty split.)

One of the factors making this result so lopsided was the termination, in December 2015, of Harold Meyerson, a social democrat and the only regular *Post* op-ed personality who might have been expected to support Sanders consistently. Fred Hiatt, who oversees the paper's editorial page, told *Politico* that Meyerson

---

* Here is how I came to this figure. I used the Nexis electronic search service to find all *Washington Post* stories mentioning Bernie Sanders printed between January 1 and May 31, 2016, and identified as "editorial copy." Judgments of what constituted "negative" and "positive" were entirely subjective. In arriving at this ratio of five to one, I did not count letters to the editor, articles that appeared in other sections of the paper, or blog posts, even though a number of the latter are described in this essay. Throughout, I have used print rather than online headlines (which sometimes differ for identical stories).

"failed to attract readers." Meyerson offered the magazine an additional explanation for his firing. Hiatt, he said, had blamed his unpopularity on his habit of writing about "unions and Germany"—meaning, presumably, that nation's status as a manufacturing paradise.

But the factor that *really* mattered was that the *Post*'s pundit platoon just seemed to despise Bernie Sanders. The rolling barrage against him began during the weeks before the Iowa caucuses, when it first dawned on Washington that the Vermonter might have a chance of winning. And so a January 20 editorial headlined "Level with Us, Mr. Sanders" decried his "lack of political realism" and noted with a certain amount of fury that Sanders had no plans for "deficit reduction" or for dealing with Social Security spending—standard *Post* signifiers for seriousness. That same day, the columnist Catherine Rampell insisted that the repeal of the Glass-Steagall bank regulatory act in the 1990s (an episode of which Sanders made much) "had nothing to do with the 2008 financial crisis," and that those who pined for the old system of bank regulation were just revealing "the depths of their ignorance."*

The next morning, the *Post* columnist Charles Lane piled on with an essay ridiculing Sanders's idea that there was a "billionaire

---

* In point of fact, several authoritative works on the financial crisis describe how the multistep repeal of Glass-Steagall (and the weak regulation that replaced it) set the stage for the meltdown. Nevertheless, dismissing the significance of the Glass-Steagall repeal became a standard talking point for anti-Sanders pundits, possibly because (a) that's what Hillary Clinton was saying, (b) it showed their solidarity with the many experts and politicians who had participated in the repeal of Glass-Steagall, and (c) Glass-Steagall was killed off by the very sort of universal, bipartisan consensus that the *Post* frequently cites as the model of correct policymaking.

class" that supported conservative causes. Many billionaires, Lane pointed out, are actually pretty liberal on social issues. "Reviewing this history," he harrumphed, "you could almost get the impression billionaires have done more to advance progressive causes than Bernie Sanders has."

On January 27, with the Iowa caucuses just days away, the *Post* columnist Dana Milbank nailed it with a headline: "Nominating Sanders Would Be Insane." After promising that he adored the Vermont senator, he cautioned his readers that "socialists don't win national elections in the United States." The next day, the paper's editorial board chimed in with "A Campaign Full of Fiction," in which it branded Sanders as a flimflam artist: "Mr. Sanders is not a brave truth-teller. He is a politician selling his own brand of fiction to a slice of the country that eagerly wants to buy it."

Stung by the *Post*'s trolling, Bernie Sanders fired back angrily from the campaign trail in Iowa—which in turn allowed no fewer than three of the paper's writers to report on the conflict between the candidate and their employer as a bona fide news item. Sensing weakness, the editorial board came back the next morning with yet another kidney punch, this one headlined "The Real Problem with Mr. Sanders." By now, you can guess what that problem was: his ideas weren't practical, and besides, he still had "no plausible plan for plugging looming deficits as the population ages."

Actually, that was only one of two editorials to appear on January 29 berating Sanders. The other sideswiped the senator in the course of settling a question of history, evidently one of the paper's regular duties. After the previous week's lesson about Glass-Steagall, the editorial board now instructed politicians to

"Stop Reviling TARP"—i.e., the Wall Street bailouts with which the Bush and Obama administrations tried to halt the financial crisis. The bailouts had been controversial, the paper acknowledged, but they were also bipartisan, and opposing or questioning them in the Sanders manner was hereby declared anathema. After all, the editorial board intoned:

> Contrary to much rhetoric, Wall Street banks and bankers still took losses and suffered upheaval, despite the bailout—but TARP helped limit the collateral damage that Main Street suffered from all of that. If not for the ingenuity of the executive branch officials who designed and carried out the program, and the responsibility of the legislators who approved it, the United States would be in much worse shape economically.

As a brief history of the financial crisis and the bailout, this is absurd. It is true that bailing out Wall Street was probably better than doing absolutely nothing, but to say this ignores the many other options that were available to public officials back then. All the Wall Street banks that existed at the time of TARP are flourishing to this day, since the government moved heaven and earth to spare them the consequences of the toxic securities they had issued and the lousy mortgage bets they made. The big banks were "made whole," as the saying goes. Main Street banks, meanwhile, died off by the hundreds in 2009 and 2010. And average home owners, of course, got no comparable bailout. Instead, Main Street America saw trillions in household wealth disappear; it entered into a prolonged recession, with towering unemployment, increasing inequality, and other effects that linger to this day. There has never been a TARP for the rest of us.

The columnist Charles Krauthammer went into action on January 29, too, cautioning the Democrats that they "would be risking a November electoral disaster of historic dimensions" should they nominate Sanders—cynical advice that seems even more poisonous today, after the Democratic candidate who supposedly embodied pragmatism and sober centrism led the party into just such a disaster. The columnist Ruth Marcus brought the hammer down two days later, marveling at the folly of voters who thought the Vermont senator could achieve any of the things he aimed for. Had they forgotten "Obama's excruciating experience with congressional Republicans"? The Iowa caucuses came the next day, and the editorial writer Stephen Stromberg was at the keyboard to identify the "three delusions" that supposedly animated the campaigns of Sanders and the Republican Ted Cruz alike. Namely: they had abandoned the "center," they believed that things were bad in the United States, and they perceived an epidemic of corruption—in Sanders's case, corruption via billionaires and campaign contributions. Delusions all.

And then, amazingly enough, the *Post* ran an op-ed bearing the headline "The Case for Bernie Sanders (in Iowa)." It was not an endorsement of Sanders, of course ("This is not an endorsement of Sanders," its author wrote), but instead of a continuing conversation among Democrats about important issues of the day. The people of Iowa "must make sure" that the battle between Clinton and Sanders continued, presumably by delivering a close result on caucus day. It was the best the *Post* could do, I suppose, before reverting to its customary position.

On and on it went, for month after month, a steady drumbeat of denunciation. The paper hit every possible anti-Sanders note, from the driest kind of math-based policy reproach to the lowest sort of nerd shaming—from Sanders's inexcusable failure to embrace taxes on soda pop to his awkward gesticulating during a debate with Hillary Clinton ("an unrelenting hand jive," wrote the *Post* dance critic Sarah L. Kaufman, "that was missing only an upright bass and a plunky piano").

The paper's piling up of the senator's faults grew increasingly long and complicated. Soon after Sanders won the New Hampshire primary, the editorial board denounced him and Trump both as "unacceptable leaders" who proposed "simple-sounding" solutions. Sanders was said to use the plutocracy as a "convenient scapegoat." He was hostile to nuclear power. He didn't have a specific recipe for breaking up the big banks. He attacked trade deals with "bogus numbers that defy the overwhelming consensus among economists."

This last charge was a particular favorite of *Post* pundits: David Ignatius and Charles Lane both scolded the candidate for putting prosperity at risk by threatening our trade deals. Meanwhile, Charles Krauthammer grew so despondent over the meager 2016 options that he actually pined for the lost days of the Bill Clinton presidency, when America was tough on crime, when welfare was being reformed, and when free trade was accorded its proper respect.

Ah, but none of this was to imply that Bernie Sanders, flouter of economic consensus, was a friend to the working class. Here, too, he was written off as a failure. Instead of encouraging the lowly to work hard and get "prepared for the new economy," moaned the *Post* columnist Michael Gerson, the senator was merely offering them goodies—free health care and college— in the manner of outmoded "20th century liberalism." Others took offense at Sanders's health care plan because it envisioned something beyond Obamacare, which had been won at such great cost.

This brings us to the question of qualifications, a nonissue for most voters that nevertheless caused enormous alarm among the punditry for a good part of April 2016. Columnist after columnist and blogger after blogger offered judgments on how ridiculous, how very *unjustified* it was for Sanders to suggest Clinton wasn't qualified for the presidency, and whether Clinton hadn't started the whole thing first by implying Sanders wasn't qualified, and whether she was right when she did or didn't make that accusation. Reporters got into the act, too, wringing their hands over the lamentable "tone" of the primary contest and wondering what it portended for November. Maybe you've forgotten about this pointless roundelay, but believe me, it happened; acres of trees fell so that every breathless minute of it could be documented.

Then there was Sanders's supposed tin ear for racial issues. Jonathan Capehart (a blogger, op-ed writer, and member of the paper's editorial board) described the senator as a candidate with limited appeal among black voters, who had trouble talking "about issues of race outside of the confines of class and poverty" and was certainly no heir to Barack Obama. Sanders was conducting a "magic-wand campaign," Capehart insisted on another occasion, since his demands for open primaries and easier voter registration would never be carried out. Even the inspiring story of the senator's salad days in the civil rights movement turned out to be tainted once Capehart started sleuthing. In February, the columnist examined a famous photograph from a 1962 protest and declared that the person in the picture wasn't Sanders at all. Even when the photographer who took the image told

Capehart that it was indeed Sanders, the *Post* grandee refused to back down, fudging the issue with bromides: "This is a story where memory and historical certitude clash." Clearly Sanders is someone to whom the ordinary courtesies of journalism do not apply.

Extra credit is due to Dana Milbank, one of the paper's ablest columnists, who kept varying his angle of attack. In February, he name-checked the Bernie Bros—socialist cyberbullies who were turning comment sections into pens of collectivist terror. In March, Milbank assured readers that Democrats were too "satisfied" to sign up with a rebel like Sanders. In April, he lamented Sanders's stand on trade on the grounds that it was similar to Trump's and that it would be hard on poor countries. In May, Milbank said he thought it was just awful the way frustrated Sanders supporters cursed and "threw chairs" at the Nevada Democratic convention—and something close to treachery when Sanders failed to rebuke those supporters afterward. "It is no longer accurate to say Sanders is campaigning against Clinton, who has essentially locked up the nomination," the columnist warned on the occasion of the supposed chair throwing. "The Vermont socialist is now running against the Democratic Party. And that's excellent news for one Donald J. Trump."*

The danger of Trump became an overwhelming fear as primary season drew to a close, and it redoubled the resentment toward Sanders. By this time Sanders had begun complaining

---

* The incident of the tossed chairs was cause for much clucking in *Post*-land. It was mentioned in an editorial on May 19 and referred to in at least three other stories. The legend of the thrown chairs turned out to be hugely exaggerated, while the DNC's non-neutrality during primary season was later established as fact.

about his mistreatment at the hands of the Democratic apparatus, and by so doing, it was thought, he was weakening the party before its coming showdown with the billionaire blowhard. This matter, like so many others, found columnists and bloggers and op-ed panjandrums in solemn agreement. Even the *Post* columnist Eugene Robinson, who had stayed fairly neutral through most of the primary season, piled on in a May 20 piece, blaming Sanders and his noisy horde for "deliberately stoking anger and a sense of grievance—less against Clinton than the party itself," actions that "could put Trump in the White House."

There were some important exceptions to the *Post's* war on Sanders. The paper's blogs, for instance, published regular pieces by Sanders sympathizers such as Katrina vanden Heuvel and the cartoonist Tom Toles. (The blogs also featured the efforts of a few really persistent Clinton haters.) The Sunday Outlook section once featured a pro-Sanders essay by none other than Ralph Nader, a demon figure for many of the paper's commentators. But readers of the *Post's* editorial pages had to wait until May 26 to see a really full-throated essay supporting Sanders's legislative proposals. Penned by Jeffrey Sachs, the eminent economist and professor at Columbia University, it insisted that virtually all the previous debate on the subject had been irrelevant, because standard economic models did not take into account the sort of large-scale reforms that Sanders was advocating.

It's been decades since the United States had a progressive economic strategy, and mainstream economists have forgotten what one can deliver. In fact, Sanders's recipes are supported by overwhelming evidence—notably from countries that already follow the policies he advocates. On health care, growth and income inequality, Sanders wins the policy debate hands down.

It was a striking departure from what nearly every opinionator had been saying for the preceding six months. Too bad it came just eleven days before the *Post,* following the lead of the Associated Press, declared Hillary Clinton to be the presumptive winner of the Democratic nomination.

What can we learn from reviewing one newspaper's lopsided editorial treatment of a left-wing presidential candidate?

For one thing, we learn that the *Washington Post,* that gallant defender of a free press, that bold bringer down of presidents, has a real problem with some types of political advocacy. Certain ideas, when voiced by certain people, are not merely debatable or incorrect: they are inadmissible. The ideas themselves might seem healthy. They might even be orthodox in other lands. Nevertheless, when voiced by the individuals in question, they become unacceptable.

We hear a lot these days about the dangers to speech posed by political correctness, about those insane left-wing college students who demand to be shielded from uncomfortable ideas. What I am describing here is something similar but far more consequential. It is the machinery by which the boundaries of the Washington consensus are enforced.

You will recall how, after the Nevada unpleasantness, Eugene Robinson, who claimed to share Sanders's philosophy, nonetheless condemned the candidate's criticism of the Democratic Party's nominating process as "reckless in the extreme." Impugning the party, Robinson argued, might empower Donald Trump. Looking back, however, it seems to me that the real recklessness is the idea that certain political questions are off-limits to our candidates—that they must not disparage the party machinery, that they must not "revile" the Wall Street bailouts, and so on.

Consider the circumstances in which *Post* pundits demanded that Sanders refrain from disparaging the Democratic National Committee. Hillary Clinton was not an incumbent president, and yet Democratic elected officials across the country were virtually unanimous in their support of her, President Obama was doing nearly everything in his power to secure her the nomination, and the DNC itself was more or less openly taking her side. All these players were determined (as we later learned) to make Clinton the nominee, regardless of the consequences. Maybe Sanders didn't have the story exactly right—nobody did, back then. But still: if ever a situation cried out for critique, for millions of newspaper readers screaming over the breakfast table, this was it.

Or maybe it is reckless of me to say so. Journalists these days are apparently expected to become soldiers in the political war, and so maybe people like me should weigh what we write against the possibility that it might in some way help the Republicans and their appalling leader.

This is a political way of looking at things, I suppose, but it would be more accurate to say that it is antipolitical, that it is actively hostile to political ideas. Consider once again the *Post*'s baseline philosophy, as the editorial board explained it in two February editorials. In one of them, headlined "Mr. Sanders'

Attack on Reality" (February 12, 2016), the editors denounced the candidate's "simplistic" views and argued that by advocating for better policies in certain areas, he was implicitly criticizing President Obama. What's the harm in that? you might wonder. No one is above criticism. The *Post* unfolded its reasoning.

> The system—and by this we mean the constitutional structure of checks and balances—requires policymakers to settle for incremental changes. Mr. Obama has scored several ambitious but incomplete reforms that have made people's lives better while ideologues on both sides took potshots.

What the *Post* is saying here is that the American system, by its nature, doesn't permit a president to achieve anything more than "incremental change." Obama did the best anyone could under this system—indeed, the paper asserted, he had "no other option" than to proceed as he did. Therefore he should be exempt from criticism at the hands of other Democrats.

The board explained its philosophy slightly differently in the other editorial, "Battle of the Extremes" (February 2, 2016). Sanders, like Ted Cruz, was said to harbor the toxic belief that "the road to progress is purity, not compromise." Again, his great failing was his refusal to acknowledge the indisputable rules of the game. Heed the wisdom of our savviest political journalists.

> Progress will be made by politicians who are principled but eager to shape compromises, to acknowledge that they do not have a monopoly on wisdom and to accept incremental change. That is a harder message to sell in primary campaigns, but it

is a message far likelier to produce a nominee who can win in November—and govern successfully for the next four years.

To say that this gets reality wrong—that there are many examples of sweeping political achievement in U.S. history, that even the most ideological politicians sometimes compromise, or that Bernie Sanders (unlike Ted Cruz) actually works well with his Senate colleagues—is only to begin unpacking the errors here. What matters more, for our purposes, is the paper's curious, unrelenting logic. Since sweeping change is structurally impossible, the *Post* assures us, no such change should be advocated by political candidates. "No we can't" turns out to be the iron law of American politics, and should therefore become the slogan of every aspiring presidential candidate.

Let's say that it's true, as the *Post* asserts, that the American system won't allow a president to achieve high-flown goals—that such accomplishments are simply out of reach, even to a golden-tongued orator or an LBJ-style political animal. Okay. But what's the harm in a candidate who *talks* about those goals? By the paper's own definition, there's no chance of them ever becoming law. The only person to be penalized for making such grand, hollow promises will be the promiser himself, whose followers will be disappointed with him after he foolishly demands a hundred percent of everything ("purity, not compromise") and is inevitably defeated by the system.

Indeed, this logic, applied across the board, would require us to condemn even the most pragmatic leaders. What are we to make, for example, of a politician who says we ought to enact some sort of gun control? Everyone knows that there is virtually no way such a measure will get through Congress, and even if it did, there's the Supreme Court and the Second Amendment to contend with. By the *Post*'s logic, that means the gun issue shouldn't even be discussed. How about a politician who goes to China and bravely proclaims that "women's rights are human rights," when all the wised-up observers know the Chinese system is organized to ensure that such an ideal will not be realized there anytime soon? And shouldn't the *Post* have frothed with vituperation at the lèse-majesté of a candidate who once confronted a respected U.S. senator with the suggestion that politics ought to be the "art of making what appears to be impossible possible"?

The reason so many *Post* pundits automatically embrace incrementalism, I think, is that it allows them to avoid taking difficult issues seriously. Bernie Sanders ran for the presidency by proposing reforms that these prestigious commentators, for whatever reason, found distasteful. Rather than grapple with his ideas, however, they simply blew the whistle and ruled them out of bounds. Plans that were impractical, proposals that would never pass Congress—these things are off the table, and they are staying off.

Clinging to this so-called pragmatism is also professionally self-serving. To recognize "realism" as the ultimate trump card in American politics automatically prioritizes the thoughts and observations of the realism experts—also known as the *Washington Post* and its brother institutions of insider knowledge and professional policy practicality. Realism is what these organizations deal in; if you want it, you must come to them. Legitimacy is their property. They dole it out as they see fit.

Think of all the grand ideas that flicker in the background of the Sanders-denouncing stories I have just recounted. There is the admiration for consensus, the worship of pragmatism and bipartisanship, the contempt for populist outcry, the repeated equating of dissent with partisan disloyalty. And think also of the loser ideas this pragmatism engendered: the cheers for TARP, the indignant refusal to question the DNC, the dismissal of single-payer health care as a preposterous dream. Why are worshipers of competence often so incompetent?

What I am describing, of course, is the ideology of the professional class, of sound-minded East Coast strivers, fresh out of Princeton or Harvard, eagerly quoting as "authorities" their peers in the other professions, whether economists at MIT or analysts at Credit Suisse or political scientists at Brookings. This ideology constantly reassures us that the experts who head up our system of government have everything well under control. Above all, it is an insider's ideology, a way of thinking that comes from a place of economic security and takes a view of the common people that is distinctly patrician.

Now, here's the mystery. As a group, journalists *aren't* economically secure. The boom years of journalistic professionalization are long over. Newspapers are museum pieces today, every bit as much as Bernie Sanders's New Deal policies. The newsroom layoffs never end: in 2014 alone, 3,800 full-time editorial personnel got the ax, and the bloodletting continues right up to the present, with the Gannett newspaper chain announcing yet another series of job cuts. Book review editors are such rare specimens that they may disappear completely, unless somebody starts breeding them in captivity. The same thing goes for the journalists who once covered police departments and city government.

At some papers, opinion columnists are expected to have day jobs elsewhere, and copy editors have largely gone the way of the great auk.

In other words, no group knows the story of the dying middle class more intimately than journalists. So why do the people at the very top of this profession identify themselves with the smug, the satisfied, the powerful? Why in the world would a person working in a moribund industry compose a paean to the Wall Street bailouts? Why would someone like the *Post* opinion writer Stephen Stromberg drop megatons of angry repudiation on a certain Vermont senator for his "outrageous negativity about the state of the country"? For the country's journalists—Stromberg's colleagues, technically speaking—that state is pretty goddamn negative.

Maybe it's something about journalism itself. This is a field, after all, that has to a pathological degree embraced the forces that are killing it. No institution has a greater appetite for trendy Internet thinkers than journalism schools. We are all desperately convincing ourselves that we need to become entrepreneurs, or to get ourselves attuned to the digital future—the future, that is, as it is described for us by a cast of transparent bullshit artists. When the TV comedian John Oliver did a riff on the tragic decline of newspaper journalism, just about the only group in America that didn't like it was—that's right—the Newspaper Association of America, which didn't think we should be nostalgic about the days when its members were successful. Truly, we are like buffalo nuzzling the rifles of our hunters.

Or maybe the answer is that people at the top of the journalism hierarchy don't really identify with their plummeting peers. Maybe the members of the D.C. punditburo think they will never suffer the same fate as, say, the *Tampa Tribune.* And maybe they're right. As I wrote this story, I kept thinking back to *Sound and Fury,* a book that Eric Alterman published in 1992, when the power of pundits was something new and slightly alarming. Alterman suggested that the rise of the commentariat was dangerous, since it supplanted the judgment of millions with the clubby perspective of a handful of make-believe experts. When he wrote that, of course, newspapers were doing great. Today they are dying, and as they gutter out, one might expect the power of this phony aristocracy to diminish as well. Instead, the opposite has happened: as serious journalism dies, Beltway punditry goes from strength to strength.

It was during that era, too, that the old-school *Post* columnist David Broder gave a speech deploring the rise of journalistic insiders, who were too chummy with the politicians they were supposed to be covering. This was, he suggested, not only professionally questionable. It also bespoke a fundamental misunderstanding of the journalist's role as gadfly and societal superego.

> I can't for the life of me fathom why any journalists would want to become insiders, when it's so damn much fun to be outsiders—irreverent, inquisitive, impudent, incorrigibly independent outsiders—thumbing our nose at authority and going our own way.

Yes, it's fun to be an outsider, but it's not particularly remunerative. As the rising waters inundate the Fourth Estate, it is increasingly obvious that becoming an insider is the only way to hoist yourself above the deluge. Maybe that is one reason why the *Washington Post* attracted the fancy of the megabillionaire Jeff

Bezos, and why the *Post* seems to be thriving, with a fancy new office building on K Street and a swelling cohort of young bloggers ravening to be the next George Will, the next Sid Blumenthal. It remains, however precariously, the cradle of the punditocracy.

Meanwhile, between journalism's insiders and its outsiders—between the ones who are rising and the ones who are sinking—there is no solidarity at all. Here in the capital city, every pundit and every would-be pundit identifies upward, always upward. We cling to our credentials and our professional-class fantasies, hobnobbing with senators and governors, trading witticisms with friendly cabinet officials, helping ourselves to the champagne and lobster at the reception. Everyone wants to know our opinion, we like to believe, or to celebrate our birthday, or to find out where we went for cocktails after work last night.

Until the day, that is, when you wake up and learn that the tycoon behind your media concern has changed his mind and everyone is laid off and that it was never really about you in the first place. Gone, the private office or award-winning column or cable news show. The checks start bouncing. The booker at MSNBC stops calling. And suddenly you find that you are a middle-aged maker of paragraphs—of useless things—dumped out into a billionaire's world that has no need for you and doesn't really give a damn about your degree in comparative literature from Brown. You start to think a little differently about universal health care and tuition-free college and Wall Street bailouts. But of course it is too late by then. Too late for all of us.

(2016)

PART 4

THE EXPLOSION

Why Millions of Ordinary Americans Support Donald Trump

Let us now address the greatest American mystery at the moment: what motivates the supporters of Republican presidential candidate Donald Trump?

I call it a mystery because the working-class white people who make up the most noticeable part of Trump's fan base show up in amazing numbers for the candidate, filling stadiums and airport hangars, but their views, by and large, do not appear in our prestige newspapers. These publications take care to represent demographic categories of nearly every kind on their opinion pages, but "blue collar" is one they persistently overlook. The views of working-class people are so foreign to that universe that when the *New York Times* writer Nick Kristof wanted to "engage" a Trump supporter for his column of March 2, 2016, he made one up, along with this imaginary person's responses to his questions.

When members of the professional class wish to understand the working-class Other, what they traditionally do is consult experts on the subject. And when these authorities are asked to explain the Trump movement, they always seem to zero in on one main accusation: bigotry. Only racism, they tell us, is capable of powering a movement like Trump's, which is blowing through the inherited structure of the Republican Party like a tornado through a cluster of McMansions.

Trump himself provides rather excellent evidence for this finding. The man is an insult clown who has systematically gone down the list of American ethnic groups and antagonized them each in turn. He wants to deport millions upon millions of undocumented immigrants. He wants to bar Muslims from visiting the United States. He admires various foreign strongmen and dictators, and has even retweeted a quote from Mussolini. This gold-plated buffoon has in turn drawn the enthusiastic endorsement of leading racists from across the spectrum of intolerance, a gorgeous mosaic of haters, each of them quivering excitedly at the prospect of getting a real, honest-to-god bigot in the White House.

This stuff is so insane, so wildly outrageous, that the commentariat has deemed it to be the entirety of the Trump campaign. Trump appears to be a racist, so racism must be what motivates his armies of followers. And so, on March 4, 2016, the *New York Times* columnist Timothy Egan blamed none other than "the people" for Trump's racism: "Donald Trump's supporters know exactly what he stands for: hatred of immigrants, racial superiority, a sneering disregard of the basic civility that binds a society."

Stories marveling at the stupidity of Trump voters are

published nearly every day. Articles that accuse Trump's followers of being bigots have appeared by the hundreds, if not
the thousands. Conservatives have written them; liberals have
written them; impartial professionals have written them. The
headline of a *Huffington Post* column from March 2, 2016,
announced, bluntly, that "Trump Won Super Tuesday Because
America Is Racist." A *New York Times* reporter proved that Trump's
followers were bigots by coordinating a map of Trump support
with a map of racist Google searches. Everyone knows it: Trump's
followers' passions are nothing more than the ignorant blurt-
ings of the white American id, driven to madness by the presence
of a black man in the White House. The Trump movement is
a one-note phenomenon, a vast surge of race hatred. Its parti-
sans not only are incomprehensible, they are not really worth
comprehending.

Or so we're told. A while ago, I sat down and watched several
hours of Trump speeches for myself. I saw the man ramble and
boast and threaten and even seem to gloat when protesters were
ejected from the arenas in which he spoke. I was disgusted by
these things, as I have been disgusted by Trump for twenty
years. But I also noticed something surprising. In each of the
speeches I watched, Trump spent a good part of his time talking about an entirely legitimate issue, one that could even be
called left-wing.

Yes, Donald Trump talked about trade. In fact, to judge by
how much time he spent talking about it, trade may be his single
biggest concern. Not white supremacy. Not even his plan to build
a wall along the Mexican border, the issue that first won him

political fame. He did it again during the primary debate on March 3, 2016: asked about his political excommunication by Mitt Romney, he chose to pivot and talk about . . . trade.

It seems to obsess him: the destructive free-trade deals our leaders have made, the many companies that have moved their production facilities to other lands, the phone calls he will make to those companies' CEOs in order to threaten them with steep tariffs unless they move back to the United States.

In the speeches I watched, Trump would sometimes embellish this vision with another favorite left-wing idea: under his leadership, the government would "start competitive bidding in the drug industry." ("We don't competitively bid!" he marveled—a true fact, a legendary boondoggle brought to you by the George W. Bush administration.) Trump extended the critique to the military-industrial complex, describing how the government is forced to buy lousy but expensive airplanes thanks to the power of industry lobbyists.

Thus did he hint at his curious selling proposition: because he is personally so wealthy, a fact about which he loves to boast, Trump himself is unaffected by business lobbyists and donations. And because he is free from the corrupting power of modern campaign finance, famous deal-maker Trump can make deals on our behalf that are "good" instead of "bad." The chance that he will actually do so, of course, is small. He appears to be a hypocrite on this issue as well as so many other things. But at least Trump is saying this stuff.

All this surprised me because, for all the articles about Trump I had read in recent months, I didn't recall trade coming up very often, if at all. Trump is supposed to be on a one-note

crusade for whiteness. Could it be that all this trade talk is a
key to understanding the Trump phenomenon?

Trade is an issue that polarizes Americans by socioeconomic status. To the professional class, which encompasses the vast majority of our media figures, economists, Washington officials, and
Democratic power brokers, what they call free trade is something
so obviously good and noble it doesn't require explanation or
inquiry or even thought. Republican and Democratic leaders
alike agree on this, and no quantity of facts can move them
from their Econ 101 dream.

To the rest of America, trade means something very different.
There is a video going around on the Internet that shows a room
full of workers at a Carrier air-conditioning plant in Indiana
being told by an officer of the company that the factory was
moving to Monterrey, Mexico, and that they were all going to
lose their jobs.

As I watched it, I thought of all the arguments over trade
that we've had in this country since the early 1990s, all the sweet
words from our economists about the scientifically proven benev-
olence of free trade, all the ways in which our newspapers mock
people who say that treaties like the North American Free Trade
Agreement allow companies to move jobs to Mexico.

Well, here was a video of a company moving jobs to Mexico,
courtesy of NAFTA. This is what it looks like. The Carrier executive talks in that familiar and highly professional HR language about the need to "stay competitive" and "the extremely
price-sensitive marketplace." A worker shouts "Fuck you!" at

the executive. The executive asks people to please be quiet so he can "share" his "information." His information about all of them losing their jobs.

Now, I have no special reason to doubt the suspicion that Donald Trump is a racist. Either he is one or (as the comedian John Oliver puts it) he is pretending to be one, which amounts to the same thing. And there is no denying the jolt of energy he has given the racist right.

But there is another side to the Trump phenomenon. A map of his support may coordinate with racist Google searches, but it coordinates even better with deindustrialization and despair, with the zones of economic misery that thirty years of Washington's free-market consensus have brought the rest of America.

It is worth noting that in his stump speeches, Trump often makes a point of assailing that Indiana air-conditioning company from the video. What this suggests is that he's telling a tale as much about economic outrage as it is of racism on the march. Many of Trump's followers are bigots, no doubt, but many more are probably excited by the prospect of a president who seems to mean it when he denounces our trade agreements and promises to bring the hammer down on the CEO who fired you and wrecked your town.

Here is the most salient supporting fact: when people actually talk to white, working-class Trump supporters, as opposed to imagining what they might say, they find that what most concerns these people is the economy and their place in it. I am referring to a study published by Working America, a political-action auxiliary of the AFL-CIO, which interviewed some sixteen hundred white working-class voters in the suburbs of Cleveland and Pittsburgh in December 2015 and January 2016.

Support for Donald Trump, the group found, ran strong among these people, even among self-identified Democrats, but not because they are all pining for the return of the Jim Crow regime. Their favorite aspect of Trump was his "attitude," the blunt and forthright way he talks. As far as issues are concerned, "immigration" placed third among the matters such voters care about, far behind their number one concern: "good jobs / the economy."

"People are much more frightened than they are bigoted," is how the findings were described to me by Karen Nussbaum, the executive director of Working America. The survey "confirmed what we heard all the time: people are fed up, people are hurting, they are very distressed about the fact that their kids don't have a future" and that "there still hasn't been a recovery from the recession, that every family still suffers from it in one way or another."

Tom Lewandowski, the president of the Northeast Indiana Central Labor Council in Fort Wayne, puts it even more bluntly when I asked him about working-class Trump fans. "These people aren't racist, not any more than anybody else is," he says of Trump supporters he knows.

When Trump talks about trade, we think about the Clinton administration, first with NAFTA and then with [Permanent Normal Trade Relations] China, and here in northeast Indiana, we hemorrhaged jobs. They look at that, and here's Trump talking about trade, in a ham-handed way, but at least he's representing emotionally. We've had all the political establishment standing behind every trade deal, and we endorsed some of these people, and then we've had to fight them to get them to represent us.

Let us linger over the perversity. Left parties the world over were founded to advance the fortunes of working people. But our left party in America—one of our two monopoly parties—chose long ago to turn its back on these people's concerns, making itself instead into the tribune of the enlightened professional class, a "creative class" that makes innovative things like derivative securities and smartphone apps. The working people that the party used to care about, Democrats figured, had nowhere else to go, in the famous Clinton-era expression. The party just didn't need to listen to them any longer.

What Lewandowski and Nussbaum are saying, then, should be obvious to anyone who's dipped a toe outside the prosperous enclaves on the two coasts. Ill-considered trade deals and generous bank bailouts and guaranteed profits for insurance companies but no recovery for average people, ever—these policies have taken their toll. As Trump says, "We have rebuilt China and yet our country is falling apart. Our infrastructure is falling apart . . . Our airports are, like, Third World."

Trump's words articulate the populist backlash against liberalism that has been building slowly for decades and that may very well come to occupy the White House itself, whereupon the entire world will be required to take seriously its demented ideas.

Yet still we cannot bring ourselves to look the thing in the eye. We cannot admit that we liberals bear some of the blame for its emergence, for the frustration of the working-class millions, for their blighted cities and their downward spiraling lives. So much easier to scold them for their twisted racist souls, to close our eyes to the obvious reality of which Trumpism is just a crude and ugly expression: that neoliberalism has well and truly failed.

(2016)

Rendezvous with Oblivion

A while ago I tried to write a column proposing mean nicknames for president-elect Donald Trump, on the grounds that it would be funny to turn the tables on him for the cruel diminutives he applied to others.

I couldn't pull it off. There is a darkness about Trump that negates that sort of humor: a folly so bewildering, an incompetence so profound that no insult could plumb its depths.

He has run one of the lousiest presidential campaigns ever. In saying so I am not referring to his much-criticized business practices or his vulgar remarks about women. I mean this in a purely technical sense: this man fractured his own party. His

---

I wrote this essay the week before the 2016 election. I turned it in on November 6 and the *Guardian* newspaper posted it a few minutes after Donald Trump was declared the winner.

convention was a fiasco. He had no ground game to speak of. The list of celebrities and pundits and surrogates taking his side on the campaign trail was extremely short. He needlessly offended countless groups of people: women, Hispanics, Muslims, disabled people, mothers of crying babies, the Bush family, and George Will–style conservatives, among others. He even lost Glenn Beck, for Pete's sake.

And now he is going to be president of the United States. The woman we were constantly assured was the best-qualified candidate of all time has lost to the least-qualified candidate of all time. Everyone who was anyone rallied around her, and it didn't make any difference. The man too incompetent to insult is now going to sit in the Oval Office, whence he will hand down his beauty-contest verdicts on the grandees and sages of the old order.

Maybe there is a bright side to a Trump victory. After all, there was a reason that tens of millions of good people voted for him, and maybe he will live up to their high regard for him. He has pledged to "drain the swamp" of D.C. corruption, and maybe he will sincerely tackle that task. He has promised to renegotiate NAFTA, and maybe that, too, will finally come to pass. Maybe he'll win so much for us (as he once predicted in a campaign speech) that we'll get sick of winning.

But let's not deceive ourselves. We aren't going to win anything. What happened on Election Day is a disaster, both for liberalism and for the world. As President Trump goes about settling scores with his former rivals, picking fights with other countries, and unleashing his special deportation police on this group and that, we will all soon have cause to regret his ascension to the presidential throne.

What we need to focus on now is the obvious question: What the hell went wrong? What species of cluelessness guided our Democratic leaders as they went about losing what they told us was the most important election of our lifetimes?

Start at the top. Why, oh why, did it have to be Hillary Clinton? Yes, she has an impressive résumé; yes, she worked hard on the campaign trail. But she was exactly the wrong candidate for this angry, populist moment. An insider when the country was screaming for an outsider. A technocrat who offered fine-tuning when the country wanted to take a sledgehammer to the machine.

She was the Democratic candidate because it was her turn and because a Clinton victory would have moved every Democrat in Washington up a notch. Whether or not she would win was always a secondary matter, something that was taken for granted. Had winning been the party's number one concern, several more suitable candidates were ready to go. There was Joe Biden, with his powerful plainspoken style, and there was Bernie Sanders, an inspiring and largely scandal-free figure. Each of them would probably have beaten Trump, but neither of them would really have served the interests of the party insiders.

And so Democratic leaders made Hillary their candidate even though they knew about her closeness to the banks, her fondness for war, and her unique vulnerability on the trade issue—each of which Trump exploited to the fullest. They chose Hillary even though they knew about her private email server. They chose her even though some of those who studied the Clinton Foundation suspected it was a sketchy proposition.

To try to put over such a nominee while screaming that the Republican is a right-wing monster is to court disbelief. If Trump is a fascist, as liberals often said, Democrats should have put in their strongest player to stop him, not a party regular they'd chosen because it was her turn. Choosing her indicated either that Democrats didn't mean what they said about Trump's riskiness, or that their opportunism took precedence over the country's well-being, or maybe both.

Clinton's supporters among the media didn't help much, either. It always struck me as strange that such an unpopular candidate enjoyed such robust and unanimous endorsements from the editorial and opinion pages of the nation's papers, but it was the quality of the media's enthusiasm that really harmed her. With the same arguments repeated over and over, two or three times a day, with nuance and contrary views all deleted, the act of opening the newspaper started to feel like tuning in to a Cold War propaganda station. Here's what it consisted of:

- Hillary was virtually without flaws. She was a peerless leader clad in saintly white, a super-lawyer, a caring benefactor of women and children, a warrior for social justice.
- Her scandals weren't real.
- The economy was doing well / America was already great.
- Working-class people weren't supporting Trump.
- And if they were, it was only because they were botched humans, beyond redemption. Racism was the only conceivable reason for lining up with the Republican candidate.

How did the journalists' crusade fail? The Fourth Estate came together in an unprecedented professional consensus. They chose insulting the other side over trying to understand what motivated them. They transformed opinion writing into a vehicle for high moral boasting. What could possibly have gone wrong with such an approach?

Put this question in slightly more general terms and you are confronting the single great mystery of 2016. The American white-collar class just spent the year rallying around a super-competent professional (who, it turns out, really wasn't all that competent) and either insulting or silencing everyone who didn't accept their assessment. And then they lost. Maybe it's time to consider whether there's something about ear-splitting self-righteousness, shouted from a position of high social status, that turns people away.

The even larger problem is that a chronic complacency has been rotting American liberalism for years, a hubris that tells Democrats they need do nothing different, they need deliver nothing really to anyone—except their friends on the Google jet and those nice people at Goldman. The rest of us are treated as though we have nowhere else to go and no role to play except to vote enthusiastically on the grounds that these Democrats are the "last thing standing" between us and the end of the world. It is a liberalism of the rich, it has failed the middle class, and now it has failed on its own terms of electability. The time is up for these comfortable Democrats and their cozy Washington system. Enough is enough.

How the Democrats Could Win Again,
If They Wanted

What made 2016 a disaster for Democrats was not merely the party's epic wipeout in Washington and the state capitals, but that the contest was fought out on a terrain that should have been favorable to them. This was an election about social class—about class-based grievances—and yet the Party of the People blew it. How that happened is the question of the year, just as it has been the question of other disastrous election years before. And just like before, I suspect the Democrats will find all sorts of reasons to take no corrective action.

But first let us focus on the good news arising from the election. Donald Trump has proven that anything is possible in politics. He has destroyed the core doctrine of Clintonism: that all elections are decided by money and that therefore Democrats must match Republican fund-raising dollar for dollar. This is the creed on which progressive hopes have been sacrificed for decades, and now it is dead. Hillary Clinton outspent Trump two to one and it still wasn't enough.

Neither were any of the other patented maneuvers of Clintonism. With Hillary carrying their banner, the Democrats triangulated themselves in every way imaginable. They partied with the Wall Street guys during their convention in Philadelphia, they got cozy with the national security set, they reached out to disaffected Republicans, they reminisced about the days of the balanced federal budget, they even encouraged Democratic delegates to take Ubers back and forth from the convention to show how strongly Democrats approved of what Silicon Valley was doing to America. And still they lost.

This is important because winning is supposed to be the raison d'être of centrism. Over the years, the centrists have betrayed the Democratic Party's liberal base in all sorts of ways— deregulating banks, securing free trade deals, signing off on Wall Street bailouts and the Iraq War. Those who bridled at all this were instructed to sit down and shut up because the pragmatists were the ones who would bring us victory.

Except that they didn't. This time the Republicans chose an honest-to-god scary candidate, a man who really ought to have been kept out of the White House, and the party's centrists choked. Instead of winning, the pragmatists delivered Democrats to the worst situation they've been in for many decades, with control of no branch of the federal government and of only a handful of state legislatures. Over the years, and at the behest of this faction, Democrats gave up what they stood for piece by piece, and what they have to show for it now is nothing.

Another shibboleth that went down with the Clinton *Titanic*

is the myth of the moderate swing voter, the sensible subur-
banite who stands somewhere between the two parties and
whose views determine all elections. These swing voters are
usually supposed to be liberal on social issues and conservative
on economic ones, and their existence gives a kind of pseudoscientific imprimatur to Democratic centrism.

For years people have pointed out that this tidy geometry
doesn't really make sense, and today it is undeniable: the real
swing voters are the working-class people who over the years
have switched their loyalty from the Democrats to Trump's
Republicans. Their views are pretty much the reverse of the standard model. On certain matters they are open to conservative
blandishments; on economic issues, however, they are pretty
far to the left. They don't admire free trade or balanced budgets or entitlement reform—the signature issues of neoliberal
centrism—they hate those things. And if Democrats want to
reach them, they will have to turn away from the so-called center
and back to the economic left.

There are some indications that Democratic politicans have
finally understood this. Elizabeth Warren's star is on the rise.
Bernie Sanders is touring the country and reminding people that
class politics are back whether we like it or not.

But the media and political establishments, I suspect, will have
none of it. They may hate Donald Trump, but they hate economic
populism even more. If history is a guide, they will embrace
any sophistry that assures them that the Democrats do not need to
broaden their appeal to working-class voters. They will blame
Sanders for Clinton's loss. They will decide that working-class

people cannot be reasoned with and so it is pointless to try. They will declare—are already declaring—that any Democratic effort to win over working-class voters is a capitulation to racism. Better to lose future elections than to compete for the votes of those who spurned their beloved candidate.

And so, before too many fund-raising dinners have been digested, they will have concluded that they don't need to worry, that demographics will bail them out sooner or later, and that the right and noble course of action is to proceed as before.

This will happen because what leading liberals cannot understand—what they are psychologically blocked from understanding—is that the problem isn't really the white working class. The problem is them.

Let me explain what I mean by reminding you what our modern form of liberalism looks like. Somewhere in a sunny corner of the country, either right now or very shortly, a group of tech tycoons or well-meaning private equity investors will meet to discuss what went wrong in this election cycle. They will consider many things: the sexism and racism of Trump voters, the fundamental foreignness of the flyover, the problems one encounters when dealing with evangelicals. They will celebrate some activist they learned about from NPR, they will enjoy some certified artisanal cuisine, they will hand out prizes to the same people who got prizes at the last event they attended, and they will go back to their comfortable rooms at the resort and sleep ever so soundly.

These people think they know what liberalism includes and what it doesn't include. And in the latter category fall the concerns that made up the heart and soul of liberal politics a few decades ago: labor and work and exploitation and economic power.

To dedicate yourself to concerns like these today is to sign up for a life of obscurity and frustration. It's to inhabit a world without foundation grants, without appearances on MSNBC, and without much job security. Nothing about this sphere of progressive activism is fashionable or attractive. Strikes drag on for weeks before they are noticed by the national media. Labor organizers are some of the hardest-working but least-thanked people I know. Labor reporters are just about extinct. Promises to labor unions are canceled almost as soon as they leave a politician's lips.

It seems clear that if rich liberals had heeded the concerns of the people I am describing, Donald Trump would not be president today. But does that mean they will change their ways now?

Put the question slightly differently: Will the *Washington Post* or the *New York Times* take the sad fate of Democratic centrism as a signal to bring a whole new vision to their op-ed pages? Will the think tanks and pressure groups of Washington finally be told by their donors: we're shifting your grant money to people who care about deindustrialization?

Of course not. Liberalism today is an expression of an enlightened professional class, and their core economic interests simply do not align with those of working people. If coming up with a solution to what ails liberalism means heeding the voices of people who aren't part of the existing nonprofit/journalistic in-group, then there will be no solution.

If the unreconstructed Democratic Party is to be saved, I suspect, what will save it is what always saves it: the colossal incompetence of the Republicans. This, too, we can already see coming down the rails. Donald Trump is getting the wrecking crew back together, and before too long, I suspect, he will have the country pining for Hillary Clinton.

(2016)

Main Street USA

Liberal Americans like to think we know the answer to a lot of things, including why those who live outside liberal bubbles chose Donald Trump for president.

Small-town people, we like to think, are Republican people. At their best, they are pious, respectful, and conservative; at their worst they are smug and self-righteous, small-minded and yet capable of broad prejudice. People in the hinterlands are different: all the adults are churchgoing puritans with a neatness obsession, and all the kids long to escape to L.A. and finally be themselves.

But there's another way of looking at it, and it starts with this fact: many small towns are dying.

Donald Trump doesn't really reflect the moral values of middle America. He is a consummate city slicker, a soft-handed, foul-mouthed toff who lives in a fifty-eight-story building and has been identified with New York City excess his entire life. But people in rural areas are desperate these days. Many of them chose Trump, despite his vulgarity and his big-city ways, because he promised to make them "great again."

Watching movies about life in small towns won't help you to understand this. You need to see rural America itself. And what you will discover, should you choose to undertake this mission in the part of the Midwest where I come from, is entirely predictable. Unless the town you choose to visit has a big public facility of some kind—a prison, for example—what you will see is ruination.

With a few exceptions, the shops on Main Street will be empty or in mothballs. There will be deindustrialization and despair. Places where things used to be made will be closed down. Population growth will be negative. There will be no local newspaper, or else just a sliver of one. There will be problems with meth. There will be hundred-year-old homes that would be millionaires' palaces were they situated in popular urban areas.

And there will be Trump signs. Big ones, still standing well after the election.

One of the specific places I have in mind is the state of Missouri. It went for Trump in an overwhelming way: the fancy New York billionaire won every county except for the ones that contain the state's big cities and its college town. Certain rural counties gave him more than 80 percent of the vote.

It was not always thus. Ten or twenty years ago, Missouri was a battleground state, liable to swing either way in a national election. In 2008, it was split almost evenly between the Republican and the Democratic candidates. Barack Obama did all right in rural areas here.

Go back even further and you will find that Missouri was a reliably Democratic state, which produced politicians such as Dick Gephardt, Stuart Symington, and Harry Truman. Even the state's famous nickname—"The Show-Me State"—was partisan in its origins; it supposedly comes from a long-ago speech by a member of Congress who soliloquized as follows: "I come from a state that raises corn and cotton and cockleburs and Democrats, and frothy eloquence neither convinces nor satisfies me. I am from Missouri. You have got to show me."

These are the basic facts, and yet if you think about it, they only deepen our mystery: there was a time when hard times and despair drove rural and small-town people to the left.

So why doesn't it work that way anymore?

Let us start with a look at one of the most quintessential and representative small towns of them all: Marceline, Missouri, population 2,350, the hometown of Walt Disney. The future filmmaker arrived in Marceline with his family in 1906 and departed for Kansas City in 1910, a brief period that was nevertheless critical in forming his character.

Years later, after becoming famous, Walt Disney made his own rightward political turn, and as he did so he came to see the small Missouri town where he grew up as a repository of all that was good and wholesome about American civilization. He returned to Marceline many times in the 1950s and 1960s, and despite Missouri's preference at the time for Democrats, the town became for him a nostalgic symbol of what modern-day America had lost.

Walt Disney's biographer Neal Gabler describes the filmmaker as a "utopian who had spent a lifetime trying to re-create the communal spirit of Marceline." The utopia known as Disneyland is, in particular, a homage to Disney's idea of small-town Missouri. Visitors enter the theme park via "Main Street USA," a confection of gingerbread buildings, barbershop quartets, and old-timey trains that Disney experts agree was inspired in some way by Marceline. You might say that the town served as Disney's model in his personal bid to make America great again.

Today it is unlikely that anyone proposing to build a chain of utopian theme parks would take Linn County, Missouri— where Marceline is found—as their inspiration. These days, the place is in the grip of the cruel economic forces that are ruining small towns in all parts of the Midwest, as visitors can plainly see from a walk down its faded main drag—also now called Main Street USA. Of course, Marceline has big things going for it that other towns don't—a printing plant and a Disney museum—but the passenger trains no longer stop here. I stood by the tracks in Marceline and watched the trains roar right on past, piled high with shipping containers headed for Kansas City.

As we ponder this area's slow journey into political redness, we can rule out one thing right away: the people in these counties didn't vote the way they did because they have gradually become rich, satisfied burghers. Every prospect suggests the opposite.

As the farmer and former state legislator Wes Shoemyer told me: "If you're in a county in Missouri that doesn't have a college or a hospital, you've just watched everything disappear. Lost our coal mines, all union. We had brick plants, used to produce bricks for housing. [We] lost all the smelting, all those union jobs."

Rhonda Perry, a Missouri farmer and the program director of the Missouri Rural Crisis Center, an organization that defends the interests of family farmers, spoke to me about how so many of the state's rural voters came to side with the billionaire New Yorker. The way she sees it, what happened was not so much a matter of enthusiasm as an ugly but predictable choice.

"They were willing to overlook some of the really horrendous things about the candidate who got elected," she told me, "because he said a lot of other things about what they were feeling." Specifically, things Trump said about trade deals such as the Trans-Pacific Partnership (TPP) and how awful they are.

It surprised me to learn this. I had always thought of farmers as big fans of free trade, since the United States exports a huge amount of food. Farmers turned against Jimmy Carter because of his grain embargo on the Soviet Union, for example, and farm lobbyists are forever pushing for opening up trade with Cuba.

But these days things are different. The way Perry tells the story, family farmers are beset by a handful of immensely powerful international food companies, and the trade deals our government has been agreeing to for decades have only helped to strengthen those corporations at farmers' expense.

This thesis was confirmed in 2015, when a World Trade Organization "appellate body" shot down a U.S. supermarket rule called "country of origin labeling" (COOL), which had required meat and vegetables to be sold with a label announcing where they came from. American farmers loved the COOL law, since it gave them an obvious advantage over imported products, and here was some shadowy, pro-corporate international organization vetoing it.

Plenty of the farmers who noticed that debacle found it easy to perceive similar threats in Barack Obama's great hoped-for TPP deal, which Obama perversely insisted on pushing for even while his handpicked successor, Hillary Clinton, tried to convince voters that she opposed it.

Then there was Obama himself. None of us city folk remember it today, but in 2008 Obama was regarded as a political savior by certain aggrieved small farmers. Back then, and unlike nearly every other national politician, Obama seemed to get it: he promised to enforce antitrust laws against big food conglomerates and to do something about corporate livestock operations. "He really ran a campaign that related to agriculture," Rhonda Perry recalls. But as president he delivered very little.

In 2016, the situation was reversed. The Democrat was the one trying to persuade voters that she was a reliable friend of business, while the Republican mouthed fake outrage against heartless multinational corporations.

"People have a sense that this corporatization is out of control," Perry continued. "And they were willing to take a chance to try to rein it in and stop it, although in some ways that was a really unfortunate choice." Was she saying, I asked, that some farmers voted for Trump as a way of getting back at corporations? Yes, she replied. "Corporatization is out of control. Some people voted for Trump for that reason."

I got a slightly different taste of heartland political thinking when I sat down for breakfast in December 2016 in Macon, Missouri, a town in the county over from Marceline's, with members of the local Lions Club. The group meets regularly over red-checkered tablecloths in the back room of the Apple Basket Cafe.

The room itself, I was told, formerly housed the printing plant of the defunct local newspaper. On one wall hung the banners of all the other service clubs that now meet here: the Kiwanis, the Optimists, the Rotarians; on another was a Thomas Kinkade print. The members of the club, good-natured men of middle age, said the Pledge of Allegiance and worked on their plans to do what service clubs do everywhere: raise money for good causes.

Then we talked politics. By and large, these were men who had voted for Trump, but few of them seemed to support him in the full sense of the word. They were apprehensive about his presidency, they didn't know what to expect from it, but many of them had made the choice anyway.

Why? One of the men present told me you could summarize it with a single word: "Hillary!" Another described it with a variant on Trump's famous proposition to black voters, which these white people clearly felt applied to them, too: "Whaddaya got to lose by making a change?"

Certain predictable conservative issues came up: meddlesome government, for example. Farmers these men knew of complained bitterly about the Environmental Protection Agency. Small bankers, too, were said to feel controlled. "We don't like to be told what to do, how to do it," someone said.

But it was not all standard Republican talking points. These men groused about how big banks were able to avoid being taken over by government insurers, they used "Goldman Sachs" as verbal shorthand for wealth and influence, and I even heard complaints about billionaires controlling the state's political process.

What did crop up persistently was a disgust with the perceived moral haughtiness of liberals. More than one member of the club referred to himself as one of Hillary Clinton's "deplorables," for example. There was resentment of "Ivy League graduates" who felt entitled to "micromanage the rest of the country." The man who told me that—a fellow wearing a U.S. Army Retired cap—also told me that "if you want to be an obnoxious slob, you have a right to be one."

This right-to-obnoxiousness raises a fascinating point: these men saw liberals as loudmouthed Pharisees, intolerant moralists who demanded that the rest of the nation snap into line—a mirror image of the Church Lady stereotype liberals used to hold of conservatives.

Everyone I spoke to that morning seemed to take for granted that liberals held some kind of unfair moral- or decibel-based advantage over conservatives. Hillary voters were "the vocal ones," a man told me. "Conservatives were afraid to speak up because of criticism from liberals," he continued, "and by God, we showed them."

And then a curious note: this same individual described how, as a boy, he once shook the hand of Harry S. Truman. He had gone on an elementary school field trip to Kansas City in the 1950s, and the ex-president, then in retirement, met with his class. I asked his opinion of the liberal Democrat Truman who—

as he acknowledged—infuriated conservatives by firing General Douglas MacArthur.

"One of the best presidents we ever had," came the reply.

In walking around these small towns, it occurred to me that nostalgia must come naturally here. The greatness of the past and the dilapidation of the present are obvious with every step you take: the solid, carefully constructed buildings from the Benjamin Harrison era that are now crumbling, the grandiose swimming pool built by the Works Progress Administration under the New Deal.

There is nostalgia in Marceline's impressive Disney Hometown Museum, which carefully documents the town's relationship with the filmmaker (the folks in town were gracious enough to open the museum, which is closed in winter, especially for me). Nostalgia also in the collection of Harry Truman memorabilia that filled the parlor of the century-old house where I stayed during my visit. Nostalgia in the shop selling old stereo equipment that I wandered into during my tour. (The proprietor was actually playing a vinyl copy of Led Zeppelin's "Stairway to Heaven," the ultimate piece of classic-rock nostalgia, on one of those fancy record players from the 1970s.)

Maybe, in writing this essay, I've been like Walt Disney was in the 1950s, returning to the familiar places of his childhood and wondering what happened to America, and what happened to our democracy.

Or maybe nostalgia is itself the problem. A Democrat I met in Macon during a conversation we had about the local enthusiasm for Trump told me that "people want to go back to

Mayberry," the setting of the beloved old *Andy Griffith Show.* (As it happens, the actual model for Mayberry, Mount Airy, a bedraggled town in North Carolina, has gone all in on the Trump revolution, according to a 2017 story in the *Washington Post.*)

Maybe it's also true, as many of my liberal friends believe, that people in this part of the country secretly long to go back to the days when the Klan was riding high or when Quantrill was terrorizing the people of neighboring Kansas, or when Dred Scott was losing his famous court case. For sure, there is a broad streak of that ugliness in the Trump phenomenon.

But I want to suggest something different: that the nostalgic urge does not necessarily have to be a reactionary one. There is nothing unprogressive about wanting your town to thrive, about recognizing that it isn't thriving today, about figuring out that the mid-century, liberal way worked better.

For me, at least, that is how nostalgia often unfolds. When I drive around this part of the country, I always do so with a WPA guidebook in hand, the better to help me locate the architectural achievements of the Roosevelt years. I even used to patronize a list of restaurants supposedly favored by Harry Truman (they are slowly disappearing).

And these days, as I pass Trump sign after Trump sign, I wonder what has made so many of Harry Truman's people cast their lot with this blustering would-be caudillo, this alarming cross between Douglas MacArthur and Strom Thurmond.

Maybe what I'm pining for is a liberal Magic Kingdom, a Midwest where things function again. A countryside dotted with small towns where the business district has reasonable job-creating businesses in it. Taverns, too.

A state where the giant chain stores haven't succeeded in

putting everyone out of business. An economy where workers can form unions and buy new cars every couple of years, where farmers enjoy the protection of the laws, and where corporate management has not been permitted to use every trick available to them to drive down wages and play desperate cities off one against the other.

Maybe it's just an impossible utopia, a shimmering Frank Capra dream. But somehow I don't think so.

(2017)

America Made Great Again

Let us think the unthinkable. Let us imagine Donald Trump's potential path to reelection as president of the United States.

He is deeply unpopular, the biggest buffoon any of us have ever seen in the White House. He manages to disgrace the office nearly every single day. He insults our intelligence with his blustering rhetoric. He endorses racial stereotypes and makes common cause with bigots. He has succeeded in offending countless foreign governments. He has no idea what a president is supposed to be or do and (perhaps thankfully) he has no clue how to govern. Of the handful of things he has actually managed to achieve, nearly all are toxic.

Now: imagine his disastrous rule reaffirmed by an enthusiastic public, with four more years to insult and offend and enact even more poisonous measures. Reader, it could happen. We know it could happen because it has happened before. Widely despised presidents get themselves reelected all the time. Men who are regarded as incompetent, callow, senile, or racist sail back into office, and are even canonized as heroic figures once they retreat into the postpresidential sunset, clearing brush or painting oil portraits.

There are many paths to such rehabilitation for Trump. Imagine him, Reagan-like, lifted up on a wave of public adulation. The economy is firing on all cylinders; the ships of many nations are parading through New York harbor; the fireworks are going off overhead and Trump is announcing that *America is back, standing tall.*

Or imagine him, Dubya-like, vowing vengeance against terrorism after a dreadful attack on American soil. He picks a fight with some annoying but unrelated nation, the news media rally around him (he has finally achieved maturity as chief executive, they say), and once victory is certain, Trump lands a jet on the deck of an aircraft carrier in a cleverly tailored flight suit: MISSION ACCOMPLISHED.

I admit that at the moment, it is difficult to conceive how Donald Trump might turn that corner. Every day the circling investigators come a little closer. Every day he tweets something stupid. Every day there is a disclosure—an alleged affair with a porn star, another emoluments snafu—of the kind that would have sunk previous administrations. Besides, the presidents I mentioned above were capable politicians, advised by men and women of a certain practical cunning. Reagan and Bush both had some basic grasp of what the public traditionally wanted from its politicians and how to go about delivering it. Trump has no such understanding. His election in 2016 was little more than an obscene gesture by an angry public using the candidate as its instrument. While voters seem to be losing patience with such symbolism—at least to judge from Trump's lousy approval ratings—the man himself shows little inclination to transcend the role that first got him elected. How could the nation possibly return him to Washington for a second term?

Here is the exercise: anticipate the ways it might happen. We take for granted (perhaps incorrectly) that Trump wants to be reelected, that the job amuses or excites him enough that he desires to stay in the White House. We further assume that he is not impeached, that he does not maneuver the country into a disastrous war, that he doesn't stage (or, alternately, fall victim to) a military coup, and that he goes about campaigning for reelection by all the standard methods available to an American politician. And that he wins. Again.

For the best idea of how such a scenario might unfold, we need only look back to the late 1990s, when things were good and America was happy with its rascally chief executive, Bill Clinton. Throughout the final years of his presidency, Clinton's approval ratings hovered near the 60 percent mark, occasionally spiking up toward 70 percent. These nosebleed numbers, remember, occurred after the president was caught in his dalliance with White House intern Monica Lewinsky and while the House of Representatives was actually in the process of impeaching him. The irony of it all was lost on no one: self-righteous politicians hated Bill Clinton, but the American public loved the jolly horn dog in the Oval Office.

However, Clinton's extraordinary popularity was not merely a reaction against the Pharisees in Congress. Nor was it the individual components of Clintonism (NAFTA, say, or telecom deregulation) that had fired the imagination of the masses. No. People loved Bill Clinton first and foremost because the economy was doing so well. He had taken over the government on the heels of an ugly recession and now just look: gasoline was cheap and the stock markets were on a tear. The Dow Jones Industrial Average, which had been a little north of 3,200 when Clinton took office, passed 10,000 in March 1999. The Nasdaq—the miracle index of the decade—ascended even more dizzyingly.

Declining to mess with a good thing, the Federal Reserve kept interest rates relatively low, simultaneously stoking the euphoric culture of the New Economy. Thanks to a brand-new thing called the Internet, it was said, humankind had entered an entirely new era. Information was now perfect, the business cycle was suspended, the boom would go on forever, and the world's weak and marginalized would embrace free trade and be lifted up by the loving kindness of markets. Or whatever. The ecstatic style of the moment was so widespread that even the sober and responsible economist Kevin Hassett—now the chair of Trump's Council of Economic Advisers—coauthored a hyperventilating book called *Dow 36,000*.

It was all, of course, a bubble, not to mention a fraud and a con. It would all come apart shortly after the turn of the century in a dazzling series of corporate scandals and market crashes. And even while the bubble lasted, its benefits were lavished mainly on the wealthy. Still, there was something real about the nineties boom, something that accounted for Clinton's popularity: *wages for ordinary workers actually grew during those years.* Unemployment was so low for so long during the Clinton era that employers briefly found themselves competing for workers rather than dismissing their entreaties. In fact, the late 1990s were the only period since the early 1970s when wages for ordinary workers went up in real terms. Hence the flavor of universal prosperity that still seems to envelop the Clinton boom in the public mind.

No, the boom didn't last. And no, it wasn't really Clinton's doing. Joseph Stiglitz, the chairman of Clinton's own Council of Economic Advisers, has famously described the policy decisions that preceded the roaring economy of the late nineties as a series of "lucky mistakes." Clinton's team, in Stiglitz's telling, made wrong move after wrong move—chasing a balanced budget, deregulating banks—but by chance, things worked out for them. The day after he was elected, Clinton said he would "focus like a laser beam on this economy," and lo and behold, he seemed to deliver. The cult of Clinton was born.

That is the prelude to today.

When members of the punditburo assess Donald Trump's record as chief executive, they generally turn to his small-minded remarks, his many falsehoods, his noisy enthusiasm for white supremacists and overseas dictators. They are aware that the economy is beginning to accelerate under his watch, but that doesn't really figure into their calculations—that item they file in a separate bin. After all, as everyone knows, Trump cannot rightfully claim credit for the long, slow march back to prosperity after the last recession. He took over only a little more than a year ago, and, besides, you don't get unemployment down by picking fights with NFL players or inveighing against an imaginary immigrant crime wave.

That Trump has no right to the glory of the current boom doesn't stop him from grabbing it, however. Declaring that the robust economy had made him "unbeatable" for reelection, Trump mused in December that his slogan for 2020 might be, "How is your 401(k) doing?" Indeed, as I write this, unemployment is at its lowest level since 2000, and at one of its lowest levels ever. People who left the workforce in despair during the last recession appear to be rejoining it. Consumer confidence is high. The economy is running at what the *Wall Street Journal* calls its "full potential," meaning that actual output is equal to theoretical estimates of maximum possible output. Share prices are high, or at least they were before an unpleasant series of corrections a little while ago.

But stock ownership—even when it's done via Trump's vaunted 401(k)s—is hardly the optimal vehicle for putting money in the hands of ordinary people. That would be improved wages, which we saw briefly in the late 1990s and quite frequently in the years prior to 1973. These days, however, flat or sinking wages are a standard feature of modern-day Western economies: with unions weak and an arsenal of wage-suppression techniques in the hands of management, business booms have for many years been confined to shareholders only.

Here's where our story takes a curious turn. Trump, for all his ignorance, seems to be aware of this. Wage stagnation, a grievance usually associated with leftish economists and AFL-CIO types, was one of the big debating points for both candidates during the 2016 campaign. It was also the focus of one of Trump's great boasts. Under his presidency, he pledged, "Prosperity will rise, poverty will recede, and wages will finally begin to grow, and they will grow rapidly."

As with most Trumpian utterances, this was probably just so much bullshit. Empty syllables, vigorously pronounced, signifying nothing. After all, the people who would pay those higher wages would be Trump's billionaire pals, the same people he's appointing to his cabinet and showering with tax cuts. Higher wages would mean companies forgoing big CEO paydays and special dividends for shareholders and all that tycoon-pleasing stuff. And the obvious and direct things that government can do to help working people—raise the minimum wage or make it easier for workers to join unions—are off the table with Republicans in charge of Congress.

But here's the twist in the tale. Trump might get his wage growth anyway. The labor market is so tight that in January 2018 we learned that Walmart, a company famous for taking a hard line on employee pay, felt it had to increase its starting wage from $9 per hour to $11. (Republicans immediately took credit for this development, of course.) A story in the *New York Times* in that same month pointed out that employers in Wisconsin were so desperate to find workers that they were hiring convicted criminals straight out of prison. The possibility of an uptick in wages was convincing enough to cause a sharp correction in stock prices a little while later.

What these news items suggest is that, given where we are, it won't take much to make this economy work for ordinary people. Or appear to work, anyway. Even a small stimulus would do it. Donald Trump quite likely understands this, along with the connection between wage growth and Bill Clinton's route to presidential popularity. Even with a loutish Republican Congress, there are plenty of things he might do to make this economy into a good one for ordinary working people—meaning just good enough for just long enough to get himself reelected. And I suspect that we will eventually see proposals of exactly this kind.

The obvious stimulus Trump might propose is his famous trillion-dollar infrastructure plan, of which he made so much on the campaign trail and which he dusted off in early 2018. Let's assume that the version of the infrastructure plan he eventually proposes is the one that dumps about 80 percent of the financing onto the private sector and state and local governments. This is far from the best way to rebuild a country's infrastructure, of course, but it would certainly have a positive (if temporary) effect on wages somewhere down the line.

Smaller stimulus efforts might also do the trick. In *Nixonland*, his celebrated history of the Vietnam era, Rick Perlstein recalls how the Nixon administration tried to improve the economy for the 1972 political season by boosting federal spending in large but noncontroversial ways. (There was, for example, the "two-year supply of toilet paper bought in one shot by the Defense Department.")

We might also see smaller, localized infrastructure programs with relatively picayune price tags but with outsized political potential. Take the various plans that are currently under way to fix the poisoned water supply of Flint, a city in the critical swing state of Michigan that for decades has been synonymous with the suffering of both the black and white working class— both of them hugely important voting blocs. Just imagine the effect, as one leading Democratic politician conjectured to me, were the Trump administration to increase those efforts in a massive way, causing an army of well-paid pipe fitters to descend on central Michigan.

The president's team could easily dream up similar mini– New Deal schemes for other deindustrialized locales in the midwestern states that are now the key to the presidency. Not only would such proposals attract Democratic votes in Congress (hey, bipartisanship!), but they would also do much to counter Trump's racist reputation—a critical consideration for someone who intends to win elections in a country that grows less white every year.

Then there is free trade. Back in 2016, when candidate Trump visited Flint, he made a caustic remark about the city's misfortunes: "It used to be that cars were made in Flint and you couldn't drink the water in Mexico. And now the cars are made in Mexico and you can't drink the water in Flint." Trump blamed this reversal on NAFTA, the original neoliberal economic deal and one of his favorite rhetorical targets while on the campaign trail.

Trump seemed to understand that trade agreements were connected to wage stagnation. ("My trade reforms will raise wages, grow jobs, add trillions in new wealth into our country," he said in a speech in Ohio in 2016.) He may or may not have understood that whatever the details of such agreements, they often furnish employers with a weapon they can brandish at working-class communities: the threat of shipping jobs overseas. Indeed, as the economy has heated up, American companies are sending jobs offshore at an ever more rapid pace.

What if Trump were to restrict that tactic, or strike some symbolic blow against it, or badmouth it in a systematic way? As it happens, NAFTA is being renegotiated right now, and we may well see Trump use those negotiations to do one or the other. The president, always a fan of burning down the village in order to save it, is currently threatening to scuttle the whole thing: "A lot of people don't realize how good it would be to terminate NAFTA because the way you're going to make the best deal is to terminate NAFTA." But even if NAFTA is mostly reaffirmed in the end, Trump could use the negotiations to dissuade employers from offshoring jobs—or merely single out some random company and hit it with substantial fines for doing so. That, too, could change the wage equation. Again: it wouldn't take much, given a business climate like the present, to have some effect.

Of course, all of this assumes that Trump's rhetoric in 2016 was sincere: that he really means to be the country's "blue-collar billionaire" and to stop what he called, in his famous (if awkward) simile, an "American carnage" of "rusted-out factories scattered like tombstones across the landscape of our nation." It also assumes that Trump knows that the interests of billionaires and those of working people are not actually in alignment with each other.*

Neither is a reasonable assumption, really. One of the deepest faiths of modern conservatism is that workers and management share some mystical bond—that what workers want more than anything is an ass-kicking billionaire as their boss, a guy who isn't afraid to growl, "You're fired." As I write this, Republicans have just finished celebrating the enactment of the Tax Cuts and Jobs Act of 2017, a colossal windfall for shareholders and corporate management that Trump pushed for on the risible grounds that

---

* One last assumption: that Trump becomes more cautious and deliberate in choosing who he insults and how he goes about insulting them, a qualification for reelection that, so far, he has shown no interest in meeting.

it would be a windfall for workers. Senator Chuck Grassley, Republican of Iowa, actually saw fit to rationalize one provision of that law with the following bouquet to middle America: "I think not having the estate tax recognizes the people that are investing, as opposed to those that are just spending every darn penny they have, whether it's on booze or women or movies."

Even so, Trump might do nothing at all and *still* get the wage growth he needs for a second term. His luck could turn out to be even better than Clinton's. After all, the forces that are causing the economy to run in high gear were set in motion years ago by Barack Obama and former Federal Reserve chair Janet Yellen. Should matters continue along this course for very much longer, Trump might be able to deliver on his promises. As I was told by Josh Bivens, an economist with the left-leaning Economic Policy Institute, "If we stick at this level of unemployment for a couple of years, you will start to see some decent wage growth."

Of course, the Fed could decide somewhere down the line that wage growth implies inflation and that interest rates must be raised—incidentally, the desired course of traditional conservatives. But in the short term, that seems unlikely. Yellen, like her predecessors Alan Greenspan and Ben Bernanke, preferred to let the economic locomotive gather speed, and when Trump nominated Jerome Powell to succeed her in November, he pointedly chose a pro-growth Yellenite instead of a conventional inflation hawk.

Some of the potential Trumpery I have just described might have real effects. Other measures would deliver a fleeting sugar high. Still others would have no impact at all, aside from appearances. But any single one of them might just be sufficient to produce the deadly phenomenon we know as Trump's reelection, while knitting together the new, faux-proletarian Republican Party that Steve Bannon used to fantasize about, that he once dreamed would "govern for a hundred years."

Before you close this book, chuckle cynically, and take a sip of bourbon, think for a second about the cultural and political delusions a roaring economy and rising wages would surely generate—just as the tech mania of the late 1990s did, and just as the bull market of the 1980s did. Perhaps Donald Trump, elevated to the presidency in 2016 as an act of protest by what he called the "forgotten men and women of our country," will actually appear to come through for them. Like Bill Clinton with his laser-like economic focus, Trump will seem to have delivered on what he promised: an economy that finally looks good for his supporters. For once, they will conclude, politics worked.

Cue the victory flotilla in New York harbor. Cue the hundred-year night.

Now, let's imagine a different scenario. Inflation is out of control. Gasoline is so expensive that the larger economy is being injured. The president, who lives to inflame society's divisions, is obviously a crook and the denials mouthed by his dwindling band of defenders convince nobody. And so a new generation of Democrats is elected to Congress in enormous numbers. This is actually what happened in 1974.

To bring the scenario up to date, let's imagine that Robert Mueller or some other investigator is quickly closing in on Trump with heaps of undeniable evidence. The Dow has stopped ascending and wages for ordinary people have gone nowhere.

More factories have rusted out. More newspapers are dead. More small towns have deteriorated, and opioids and meth are cutting even greater swathes across the hinterland. The president has achieved nothing except deregulation for polluters, angry alienation for every ethnic group in the land, and tax cuts for the rich. No one believes a word Trump says, and the American carnage mounts in great heaps of ruined lives.

In such a scenario, every bit as likely as the ones mentioned above, it seems like a cinch: Democrats will easily sweep this preposterous man and his dysfunctional, divisive party into the gutter. Besides, what will Trump promise us in 2020, when nothing has improved for ordinary people? That he still means to "drain the swamp," after essentially bathing in it for the previous four years? That he'll just need one more term to revive the faltering coal industry? That he'll Make America Even Greater Again?

Given such a setup, it might seem like a simple matter for the Democrats to defeat Trump's Republicans. The enthusiasm is certainly on their side. The liberal rank and file are more energized than they have been for years. Political novices are signing up to run for office across the country. Democrats are ahead in nearly any poll you care to mention. But still, I give them only a fair to middling chance of ultimately defeating him.

Why? Because you go into political combat with the party you have, not the party you wish you had. And the Democratic Party we have today is not particularly well suited to the essential task of beating Donald Trump.

It is true that the Democrats' fighting instincts have been aroused by the ascendancy of Trump, and this is a healthy thing. Fewer and fewer American liberals worship at the shrine of bipartisanship, as they have done for most of the last few decades. Instead, they are outraged. They are horrified at what has happened. Images of Republican governance that were formerly considered extreme are now taken for granted. That a quality person like Hillary Clinton, who prepared to be president all her life, should be bested by this vulgar, racist ignoramus—it is unthinkable. It is unacceptable.

I understand this reaction. I have felt it myself. But it has led the Democrats into a trap familiar to anyone with experience of left-wing politics: the party's own high regard for itself has come to eclipse every other concern. Among the authorized opinion leaders of liberalism, for example, the task of deploring and denouncing the would-be dictator Trump has entirely crowded out the equally important task of assessing where the Democratic Party went wrong. Indeed, the two projects appear to them to be contradictory—they find it impossible to flagellate Trump one day and to be introspective the next. Between the two, it is introspection that must hit the bricks. And it is uncompromising moral stridor that has come to dominate the opinion pages and the airwaves of the enlightened—a continuous outpouring of agony and aghastitude at Trump and his works.

This is unfortunate, because what happened in 2016 deserves to be taken seriously. This country of 320 million people was swept by a tidal wave of populist rage. In addition to the ugly gusher of bigotry that Trump tapped, there swirled perfectly legitimate concerns about deindustrialization, oligarchy, the power of big banks, bad trade deals, and the long-term abandonment of working-class concerns by the Democrats. I am condensing many strands here, of course, but what's important is that, for all its awfulness, there were elements of the 2016 revolt that liberals ought to heed.

But most leading Democrats can't seem to see any of that, however. They don't know what to make of Trump and his supporters, so violently does Trumpism transgress the professional norms to which they are accustomed. It is distasteful to them that they should be required to learn anything from a clown like the current president—that they should have to change in any way to accommodate his preposterous views. And so they cast about for leaders who might allow them to prevail without doing anything differently: a celebrity who might communicate better, a politician who might turn out the base more effectively. They devour articles about Trump voters who have had a change of heart—who now beg forgiveness for their sins. They scold liberals they regard as insufficiently enthusiatic about the Democratic Party. Above all, they dream of a deus ex machina, a super prosecutor who brings down justice like fire and reverses the unfortunate results of 2016 without anyone having to change their talking points in the slightest.

The price of going down this path is that it encourages passivity and delusions of righteousness. Their job, Democrats think, is to wait for Trump to be led out of the Oval Office in flexicuffs while they stand by anathematizing him and his supporters. They don't need to persuade anyone. They need only to let their virtue shine bright for all to see.

Now, this is a morally satisfying position no doubt, and it might even work. Maybe some prosecutor has really and truly got the goods on this scoundrel. Maybe the outpouring of anti-Trump feeling will suffice to defeat him. Lord knows Trump is deeply unpopular today; being against him may be all that voters require from a candidate in midterm congressional contests.

On the other hand, in the vast catalogue of social posturing, there are few sights more repugnant than rich people congratulating themselves for being so very, very good. In particular, it is a terrible way to win back the blue-collar white voters who were responsible, even more than were the Russians, for Trump's win. For insight into the thinking of this cohort, I turned once again to the Working America project, which canvasses working-class neighborhoods around the country. Karen Nussbaum, the organization's executive director, was blunt about it: "If Democrats just want to keep piling on Trump, that will be the way to get Trump reelected." Resisting his agenda is important, of course, but when Working America canvassers knock on doors, she added, they never point the finger at Trump voters. "We don't say, Aren't you sorry you voted for him? That's the *last* thing you should talk about with them."

The real concerns of such voters, Nussbaum told me, are such bedrock matters as jobs, wages, schools, Social Security—the very things Trump made such a loud display of pretending to care about in 2016. The Democrats, of course, did their pretending in the other direction that year. They identified themselves with globalization, with trade agreements, with booming information-age industries like Silicon Valley, addressing the public as complacent representatives of this triumphant economic order. It was an old line of patter, the philosophy of the nineties, reiterated mechanically in a time when no one believed it anymore.

Yes, the Democrats also promised to "break barriers" so that the talented could rise regardless of race or gender. The system itself, however, was judged to be in excellent health. As President Obama himself put it just before the election, "The economic progress we're making is undeniable." Or, as Hillary Clinton herself liked to say, "America never stopped being great."

It was exactly the wrong message for an enormous part of the population. Stanley Greenberg, the veteran Democratic pollster who understood the Trump phenomenon better than many others, told me recently that the Democrats' mistake was to be "selling progress at a time of growing, record inequality, stark pain, and financial struggle." Even when the Democrats could see the obvious shortcomings of such an approach, they felt they couldn't change. "How do I talk about their pain without sounding like I'm criticizing President Obama and his economy?" Hillary Clinton asked Greenberg during the campaign, according to a 2017 essay he wrote for the *American Prospect*. "I just can't do that."

That dilemma persists to this day. How do Democrats change course without sounding like they're criticizing Obama or the Clintons—or, by extension, the neoliberal fantasy that has sustained the party since the nineties? The answer is that they can't, and so they don't. They would rather sit back and expect Robert Mueller to rescue them. They would rather count on demographic change to give them a majority somewhere down the road. So they "do nothing and wait for the other side to implode," observed Bill Curry, a former adviser to President Clinton who has emerged as one of the Democratic Party's strongest internal critics. "That's been their strategy for most of my adult life. Well, how's that been working out?"

Curry continued his critique. The party, he said, desperately needed to get over its infatuation with its glorious past.

The mistakes of the Democratic Party are the mistakes of Obama and Clinton. Taking responsibility for those mistakes means holding them accountable. And so many people have such deep, positive feelings for Obama and the Clintons that they can't bear to have that conversation.

His conclusion was as blunt as what I heard from so many others: "Trump wins by the Democrats not changing."

This sounds dreadful to me, but I suspect that for certain prosperous liberals it's not such a bad choice. Their disdain for the president is sincere, of course, but it arises from a perception of impropriety, not a fear of material injury. And so for them, there's a realistic alternative to political victory: a utopia of scolding. Who needs to win elections when you can personally reestablish the rightful social order every day on Twitter and Facebook? When you can scold, and scold, and scold, and scold. That's their future, and it's a satisfying one: a finger wagging in some vulgar proletarian's face, forever.

I paint a gloomy picture here, I admit. If the economy zooms, I have conjectured, Donald Trump has a good chance of being reelected. If economic conditions don't change and Democrats play out their strategy of indignant professional-class self-admiration, they have only a fair chance of chasing him out of office—after which they will undoubtedly be surprised by some new and even more abrasive iteration of right-wing populism.

What I want to focus on now is how right-wing populism can be defeated more or less permanently. Donald Trump will never seem like a natural or inevitable president to me—not merely because he is a cad in a shockingly cantilevered ducktail, but because right-wing populism is itself a freakish historical anomaly. Yes, I know, it has been running strong for decades. By its very nature, however, it is a put-on, a volatile substance, riven with contradictions: it rails against elites while cutting taxes for the rich; it pretends to love the common people while insulting certain people for being a little *too* common; it worships the working man while steadily worsening his conditions.

Nor can I reconcile myself to the sort of prosperous, pious liberalism that predominates nowadays, a nice suburban politics that finds it easy to love Google and Goldman, but that can be downright contemptuous toward the desperate middle class that liberalism was born to serve. To my eye, the passionless technocrats it has repeatedly chosen as its leaders seem as unnatural as Trump himself.

But maybe that's just me, still dazed by what happened on election night in 2016. Nothing in politics seems right anymore. I keep assuming that a society plumbing the depths of inequality ought to be a society turning to the left—that a populist moment ought to be a Democratic moment—that the natural agent of public discontent ought naturally to be the more liberal of the two parties. One fine day, I tell myself, we will give the TV set a smack and everything will snap back into focus and Americans will clearly understand what a mountebank Trump is. That in January 2021, they will eject him from the White House in disgrace—a Herbert Hoover, a scowling mistake we will never make again.

What might Democrats do to bring that about? A while back, I used to write earnest essays exhorting Barack Obama to do this thing and that during his final years in power. Enforce antitrust! Prosecute financial fraud! Today, however, the party has no national power to demonstrate its solicitude for the crumbling middle class. Republicans have pretty much captured it all.

What is left to liberals today is positioning and public declaration. They must do the obvious, of course: find a way to capitalize on the incredible political blunders Trump has made, pointlessly disparaging this group and that. "He is pissing people off at such an accelerated rate," marvels Keith Ellison, the representative from Minnesota who serves these days as deputy chairman of the Democratic National Committee. As ugly as Trump's ravings may be, they can't help but mobilize the Democratic base.

Getting those voters out is the tactical challenge. The larger, strategic question has to do with the Democratic Party's identity. Does it accept the Republicans' invitation to continue on as it has before, making itself more and more into an expression of professional-class disdain? Friend to the enlightened financier, careful curator of the silicon millennium? Or do the Democrats rediscover their roots as the tribune of blue-collar America? For me, the answer has never been more obvious. For others as well. "Sit with some folks who work for a living," is Ellison's prescription. "Ask them what they want. And you'll win."

In 1941, President Franklin Roosevelt set down his vision of American political history, in which two "schools of political belief," liberals and conservatives, fought endlessly for primacy. Regardless of what it was called at any particular moment, he wrote, "the liberal party . . . believed in the wisdom and efficacy of the will of the great majority of the people, as distinguished from the judgment of a small minority of either education or wealth."

What Roosevelt did not foresee was a party system in which the divide fell not between the few and the many, but rather between the small minority of education and the small minority of wealth. How could he have known that his great majority would be split in two and offered a choice between enlightened technocrats on the one side and resentful billionaires on the other?

Get that great majority back together, I think, and they would be unstoppable. There is really only one set of successful politics for an age of inequality like this one, and it naturally favors the party of Roosevelt. Trump succeeded by pretending to be the heir of populists past, acting the role of a rough-hewn reformer who detested the powerful and cared about working-class people. Now it is the turn of Democrats to take it back from him. They may have to fire their consultants. They may have to stand up to their donors. They will certainly have to find the courage to change, to dump the ideology of the nineties, the catechism of tech, bank, and globe that everyone now knows is nothing but an excuse for an out-of-touch elite. But the time has come. History is calling.

(2018)

ACKNOWLEDGMENTS

The essays that make up this volume appeared in different form in the following publications between the years 2011 and 2018:

The Baffler: "Too Smart to Fail" (excerpted in the introduction), "Dead End on Shakin' Street," and "Academy Fight Song."

Harper's: "Servile Disobedience," "Home of the Whopper," "A Matter of Degrees," "Course Corrections," "Beltway Trifecta," "Bully Pulpit," "The Powers That Were," and "America Made Great Again."

Salon: "The Architecture of Inequality," "Meet the DYKWIAs," and "The Animatronic Presidency."

The Guardian: "Why Millions of Ordinary Americans Support

Donald Trump," "Rendezvous with Oblivion," "How Democrats Could Win Again, If They Wanted," and "Main Street, USA."

For purposes of this book, these essays have been edited and polished and tweaked and tightened and even updated slightly here and there to take into account later developments.

Many people helped me along the way. Specifically, I wish to thank: Chris Lehmann, George Scialabba, John Summers, and Eugenia Williamson at the *Baffler*; Ian Blair and Dave Daley at *Salon*; Rebecca Brill, Camille Bromley, Jess Cotton, Jeff Ernsthausen, Donovan Hohn, Alex Kelly, Rick MacArthur, James Marcus, Stephanie McFeeters, Ben Metcalf, Simone Richmond, Ellen Rosenbush, Daoud Tyler-Ameen, and Joe Vaccaro at *Harper's*; Amana Fontanella-Khan, Lee Glendinning, Kira Goldenberg, Jessica Reed, and David Shariatmadari at the *Guardian*.

Dean Baker, Bill Black, and James K. Galbraith were my go-to guys on all matters economy related. David Mulcahey was and is an all-around genius. Adam Johnson of FAIR helped out hugely with "The Powers That Were."

And of course Sara Bershtel and Riva Hocherman remain the best editors in the business. My agent, Joe Spieler, has represented me for years with ability and discernment.

It has been an enormous pleasure working with all of you.